The Information Please® Girls' Almanac

ILLUSTRATION CREDITS:
Body and Mind: *Brain, Chromosomes, Female Reproductive System, Female External Genitalia, Bananas* Laurel Cook Lhowe *Moon Cycle, Mother and Child* Sara Mintz Zwicker *Bathtub* Lynn Michaud *Garlic* Chris Costello **Calendar:** *Snowdrop, Violet, Daffodil, Sweet Pea, Lily of the Valley, Rose, Water Lily, Calendula* Laurel Cook Lhowe *Poppy, Morning Glory, Chrysanthemum, Poinsettia* Chris Costello **Crackerjack Kids and Careers:** *First Prize* Sara Mintz Zwicker *Julia Child* Rosemary Fox **Dating and Mating:** *Wedding Cake, Wheat, Daisies, Mule* Sara Mintz Zwicker *Children Sipping Straw, Ivy, Hand with Ring* Lynn Michaud **Fashion and Dress:** *Camisole, Jeans Pocket, Wardrobe, Bra, Pillbox Hat, Poodle Skirt, Hippie, Perfume Bottle* Sara Mintz Zwicker *Long Top over Leggings, Belly Bag, Gloves, Bike Shorts with T-Shirt, Egyptian* Lynn Michaud **Girl Talk:** *Eleanor Roosevelt* Rosemary Fox *Corn* Lynn Michaud *Topsy-turvy Doll* Sara Mintz Zwicker **Invention Convention:** *Grocery Bag, Pizza, Beaker* Sara Mintz Zwicker *Bacteria* Laurel Cook Lhowe **Making Connections:** *Cut-out Dolls, Record* Sara Mintz Zwicker **Name Calling:** *Hillary Rodham Clinton, Harriet Tubman* Rosemary Fox *Madonna* Sara Mintz Zwicker **Sports Special:** *Sneakers, Field Hockey Sticks* Lynn Michaud *Roller Skate* Chris Costello **Women of Influence:** *Susan B. Anthony Dollar, Crown* Sara Mintz Zwicker

Library of Congress Cataloging-in-Publication Data
Siegel, Alice.
The information please girls' almanac / Alice Siegel and Margo McLoone.
    p.   cm.
  ISBN 0-395-69458-2
  1. Teenage girls—Life skills guides. 2. Socialization. 3. Teenage girls—Psychology. 4. Adolescent psychology.
I. McLoone-Basta, Margo. II. Title.
HQ798.S49 1995
305.23'5—dc20
                                     95-5810
                                       CIP

Information Please is a registered trademark of Houghton Mifflin Company.

Book design by Catharyn Tivy.

Printed in the United States of America
DOH 10 9 8 7 6 5 4 3 2 1

The Information Please® Girls' Almanac

Margo McLoone and Alice Siegel

HOUGHTON MIFFLIN COMPANY
BOSTON • NEW YORK

DEDICATIONS:

For girls everywhere.

For my children, Andrew, Howard, and James. But especially for George. — A.S.

For my mother, Kathryn Daly, and my sister, Mary Kaye, who are the most extraordinary women I have known. — M.M.

ACKNOWLEDGMENTS

Thanks to the following women and girls for their strength, support, and suggestions: Catherine Basta, Liz Basta, Jenna Perrin, Simone Perrin, Annie McLoone, Stephanie Nadel, Heidi Ledet, Ginny Greendlinger, Rose Fox, Pernille Flesche, Judy Karp, Loni Larsen, Jackie Oster, Mary Jean Gilligan, Buffy Barlow, Debbie Mangan, Jean Morris, Ann Ross, Mary Ellen Aliberti, Selena Nelson, Ann Mooney, Molly McLoone, Maura McLoone, Katarina Ricken, Joan Shuman, Selena Nelson, Suzie Motzkin, Leota Davis, Teresa Rudin, Nancy McLoone, Sam Ryun, Theresa Knauth, Esther Schurnberger, Kathleen McGuiness, Jane Young, Vicky Beal, and Helen McFarlane. Thanks also to Liz and Roz of The Bookmart, Nic Harcourt of WDST, and Jane, Judy, and Joann of the Woodstock Library. Special thanks to Jeremy Perrin, Ken Linge, Bill O'Neill, Jimmy Barlow, John Melton, and Dave Ryun and to my brothers, John, Jerry, Don, Mike, and Steve. — M.M.

Special thanks to Valerie Bolling and Teresa Flaherty, teachers at Hamilton Avenue School who supplied current fashion and music information; Susan Marino, who was able to decipher my handwriting and help with the typing; Deolinda Everham for photocopying; and Jan Benedict, who is responsible for making me computer literate. A special thank you to all those behind the reference desk at the Greenwich Public Library and the Scarsdale Public Library. Finally, thanks to Steve Lewers for his faith in the book from its earliest beginnings, and to our editor, Marnie Patterson, for keeping us on track.— A.S.

Contents

Body and Mind

EVERY HUMAN BODY IS UNIQUE. How is your body different from boys' bodies on the inside and on the outside? What's it like growing up female in your culture and in other cultures? How does your mind affect your body and what can you do to feel good about your body? You'll find the answers to these questions and more in this chapter.

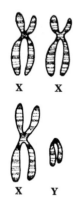

X   X

X   Y

Three out of four human sexual functions are female: menstruation, gestation, and lactation. One human sexual function is male: impregnation.

WHAT ARE LITTLE GIRLS MADE OF?

What are girls made of? Surely not sugar and spice and everything nice. Different combinations of the X and Y chromosomes make boys boys and girls girls. A girl is a girl because she has two powerful X-chromosomes. The X-chromosome is the largest of all chromosomes. Males have one X-chromosome and one Y-chromosome. Y is often the smallest chromosome. The egg, which carries all the genetic messages a child will ever receive, is several hundred times larger than the sperm that fertilizes it. Female is the original sex; every fetus begins as a female.

FEMALE EVENTS

The female body is incredible. The following list describes the events in a female's body that enable her to bear children. There are no counterparts for males. Let's explain:

- At birth, a female child has about 400,000 immature eggs, or ova, in her ovaries.
- During puberty the eggs begin to mature. Each month one egg ripens and leaves the ovary. It passes through the fallopian tube where, if not fertilized by a sperm, it disintegrates. The uterus, which has built up tissue and blood for the egg, sheds its lining about a week after the egg disintegrates. This is the event known as the menses, or menstrual period.
- *Gestation* begins when an egg that has been released from the ovary is fertilized by a male's sperm. The result is pregnancy and the eventual birth of a child.
- *Lactation* is the production of milk in a woman's

breasts to feed her newborn child.

• *Menopause* is when a woman's ovaries gradually stop functioning. This marks the end of her child-bearing years.

Female Reproductive System

Internal:

Ovaries:
The organs that hold the ova, or eggs, and where the ova ripen.

Fallopian tubes:
The passageways from the ovaries to the uterus traveled by the ripened ova.

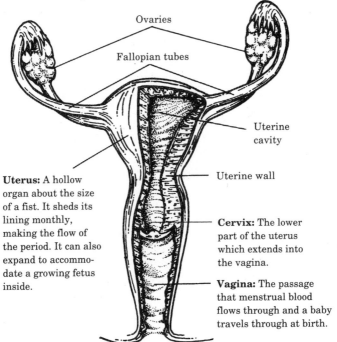

Ovaries

Fallopian tubes

Uterine cavity

Uterine wall

Uterus: A hollow organ about the size of a fist. It sheds its lining monthly, making the flow of the period. It can also expand to accommodate a growing fetus inside.

Cervix: The lower part of the uterus which extends into the vagina.

Vagina: The passage that menstrual blood flows through and a baby travels through at birth.

PMS: MYTH OR FACT?

Even though girls and women have been menstruating since the beginning of time, premenstrual syndrome—PMS—was first diagnosed in 1931. A gynecologist named Dr. Robert Frank came up with 150 symptoms that women may experience the week before their periods. These symptoms ranged from forgetfulness and clumsiness to headaches and bloating. Because many females experience some of these symptoms PMS can wrong-

Female Reproductive System

External: Vulva

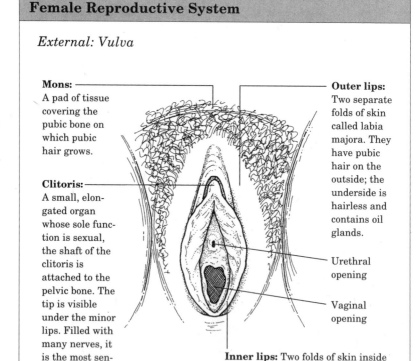

Mons:
A pad of tissue covering the pubic bone on which pubic hair grows.

Clitoris:
A small, elongated organ whose sole function is sexual, the shaft of the clitoris is attached to the pelvic bone. The tip is visible under the minor lips. Filled with many nerves, it is the most sensitive part of the female body.

Outer lips:
Two separate folds of skin called labia majora. They have pubic hair on the outside; the underside is hairless and contains oil glands.

Urethral opening

Vaginal opening

Inner lips: Two folds of skin inside the outer lips. These are called labia minor. They are also hairless and have oil glands.

fully stereotype women as irrational and unstable.

Premenstrual symptoms might include menstrual cramps, bloating, headaches, and weight gain from water retention. Some girls and women experience some of these, some experience all of them, and some do not experience any of them, but when symptoms do occur, they do so at regular intervals. A recent psychological study states: "The premenstrual mood change appears to be of the same order as afternoon lassitude, hurt feelings, or Monday morning blues....Women readily cope with premenstrual mood changes and are sometimes not even aware of them."

FROM GIRL TO WOMAN: HOW YOUR BODY CHANGES

The passage from girl to woman is called puberty. It begins for girls anywhere from age 8 to 16; the average age is 11. What happens to your body during puberty?

- You experience a growth spurt
- Your internal reproductive system matures: your ovaries and uterus grow larger
- Secondary sex characteristics appear: budding breasts and the growth of pubic hair
- Fat to muscle ratio increases
- Your voice deepens
- You begin your menses or uterine bleeding. The first menstrual periods are often irregular and infertile. You may menstruate once, then not again for several months. Your period occurs every 25 to 35 days; bleeding lasts 3 to 7 days. (The cycle begins on the day menstruation begins.)

Estrogen production increases around the twelfth day of the cycle. After the egg drops and is not fertilized, estrogen decreases and progesterone increases. Both decrease a few days after menstruation begins.

RITES OF PASSAGE IN AMERICA

Getting your period (menstruation) is a sign of maturity or coming of age—a cause for celebration. In America, coming of age ceremonies or celebrations are rare because girls are raised to think they must keep their periods a secret or talk about menstruation in code words. Many American women are now calling for a change in thinking about this natural sign of femaleness to help girls feel proud instead of embarrassed about their menstrual cycle.

Native American Ceremonies

- Among the Navajo there is a coming of age ceremony called *kinaalda*. Young girls run footraces to show their strength. They also bake a huge cornmeal pudding for the whole community to taste. During the ceremony girls wear special clothing and arrange their hair to imitate the goddess Changing Woman. Girls then reenact Changing Woman's encounter with the sun. In this skit, the beauty, skill, and labors of the goddess are honored.

- The Nootka Indians of the Pacific Northwest consider a girl's first period a time to test her physical endurance. She is taken way out to sea and left there. She must then swim back to shore on her own, where she is greeted and cheered by the whole village. The Nootka believe that physical endurance builds character.

- The Mescalero Apaches consider the female puberty ceremony the most important celebration in their tribe. Each year an eight-day event honors all the girls who started their period that

Religious ceremonies like the Jewish Bat Mitzvah and the Christian confirmation are the only rites of passage for American girls. A debutante ball is a welcoming of girls into "society."

year. It begins with four days of feasting and dancing. Boy singers recount the tribe's history with songs—64 different ones—each night. A four-day private ceremony follows, in which the girls reflect on the changes in their bodies and their passage to womanhood.

AROUND THE WORLD

Australia
Among the Aborigines of Australia, a girl is treated to the tradition of "love magic" when she gets her first period. The women of the tribe sing and teach her about the female powers and the physical changes that mark womanhood. After the love magic, the girl retreats to a secluded hut built by her mother or grandmother. After a few days of being alone, the girl is taken to a river where all the women splash and dunk her while her mother burns the seclusion hut. The girl's body is then decorated and she returns to the tribe, where she is matched with a husband.

Japan
When a Japanese girl gets her first period, her family throws a big party. Family and friends are invited but they are not told why they are celebrating. When the girl's family brings out a tray bearing either a pear decorated with leaves, a candied apple, or red-colored rice and beans, the secret reason for the party is clear to the guests.

Micronesia
The tribe of Ulithi call a girl's rite of passage *kufar*. When a girl first notices blood flow, she must go to the menstrual house. She is joined by the

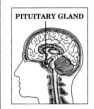

PITUITARY GLAND

The time of your first period is determined by the brain's hypothalamus. It stimulates the pituitary glands which regulate your ovaries.

The menstrual cycle is closely tied to the moon's cycle. It is a natural and rhythmic reminder of female body functions.

women of the village who bathe her and recite magic spells over her which are meant to help her find a mate. Within a month of her first period, the girl goes to live in a private hut built for her near her parents' house. She lives there until she is married, but she must always return to the menstrual house during her period.

Nigeria

The Tiv tribe literally mark a girl at the time of her first period. Four lines are cut into her abdomen. The remaining scars represent her womanhood and are thought to make her more fertile.

Sri Lanka

When a girl gets her first period in Sri Lanka, the exact time and day are noted. An astrologer is consulted who predicts many things about the girl's future based on the time and the alignment of the stars. The family then prepares their house for a ritual bathing. They whitewash the house, bake oil cakes, and put the girl in a small room where she is allowed to eat only certain foods, like rice and vegetables. A pot full of herbs is prepared and the girl is taken outside where it is poured over her head; the pot is then smashed and broken. Then the women of the family wash her hair and scrub her all over. She then puts on new white clothes from her underwear to her shoes. Printed invitations are sent for friends to attend a party where gifts and money are presented to the girl.

Zaire

When the firstborn daughter of a Mbuti Pygmy family gets her first period, she is sent to live in a menstrual hut built especially for her. Only girlfriends and women are allowed in the hut for the year she lives there. The older tribeswomen teach the girl how to avoid getting pregnant. Her friends bring her palm oil and meat to fatten her because fatness is prized in women. While the girl is in the hut, her feet are not allowed to touch the ground. Her feet are wrapped in leaves when she walks. At the end of her stay in the hut, she is painted in white clay and treated to a tribal ceremony called *elima*. At the close of the ceremony, she and her friends run through the forest singing to proclaim her womanhood.

MENSTRUAL TABOOS

Throughout history, all over the world, many societies have considered menstruation unclean. As a result, women have been confined during the time of their periods. In primitive societies, similar rules often apply: A girl who has her period must not see the sun or touch the earth, and her contact with men, animals, and food must be restricted. Primitive people believe that a woman's menstrual blood poisons the other sources of life on earth. Here are some examples of menstrual taboos:

- There is a tribe in Borneo that puts young girls in dark cells set up on posts. After a girl completes her first period she is released from the cell. Sometimes girls have to remain in the cells for many months.
- Among tribes in South America, menstruating girls lie suspended in hammocks with their faces covered so as not to see the sun.
- In New Ireland, menstruating girls are placed in dark narrow cages which are raised above the ground.

It is not unusual for menstruation to stop because of emotional stress such as shock, fear, or depression. For example, women in concentration camps did not menstruate. Menstruation will also stop if your body weight drops dangerously low. This is common among anorexic females.

15

- In South Africa, some tribes do not allow women to use the same paths as cows for fear that menstrual blood will kill the cows!

WOMEN THROUGH TIME

In the Bible, Eve lived in the Garden of Eden. She was the first woman of Judeo-Christian history. But we are all daughters and sons of a woman who lived about 200,000 years ago in Africa. Scientists have isolated one DNA "fingerprint" that is common to the whole human race and it is female; one woman is the original gene font for the whole human race.

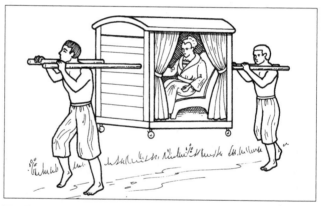

Early women were powerful, strong, and free. They controlled their bodies and those of their children. They were the leaders, the wise women, the storytellers, the doctors, the magicians, and the lawgivers in their societies. Their power to create new life, and their menstrual cycles, were held in awe by their male counterparts. But since ancient civilization, being female has become, sometimes, something very different. Here are the ways some cultures have treated the female sex:

- For thousands of years in China, preparation for childbirth included keeping a box of ashes next to the birthing bed. The ashes were used to suffocate the baby if it was a girl.
- In India, unwanted baby girls were poisoned, thrown into the sea, drowned in milk, or fed to sharks.
- The Greek philosopher Aristotle taught that women were unfinished men and that the male ruled by natural superiority.
- A nineteenth-century philosopher listed the following as the ill effects of schooling for girls: nervousness, anemia, hysteria, stunted growth, and excessive thinness. Moreover, he stated that overtaxing a girl's brain ended in flat-chested women who could not give birth to a developed infant.
- In the 1980s in China, amniocentesis, a test to determine the sex and health of a fetus, was used to abort unwanted females.
- A recent UN report stated that Third World countries provide examples of undernourished female and well-nourished male children. What food there is goes to the boys of the family rather than the girls.
- Female circumcision is common in Africa among Somalis; 98% of females have undergone the operation. Muslim women the world over must have this operation before they are allowed to marry.
- In 1994, the U.S. State Department issued a human rights report which focused for the first time on women's rights. Examples of female torture from 193 countries were cited.

The predominance of right-handedness is of female origin. From the earliest known time, women carried their babies on their left sides so the babies would feel the comfort of a beating heart. This practice left the right hand free for action.

THE WEAKER SEX? WHO SAID SO?

When the English essayist Samuel Johnson was asked who was smarter, man or woman, his response was "Which man—which woman?"

Scientists who have studied the differences between girls and boys say that there are more differences within each sex than there are differences between the sexes. These are the known body and gender differences.

The female chromosome, XX, carries genes for producing immunities from disease. Estrogen and progesterone, the female hormones, stimulate certain blood cells to destroy infectious diseases.

- From birth through puberty, girls are physically and developmentally more mature than boys.
- Boys tend to be heavier and longer at birth than girls.
- Girl babies are stronger than boy babies. Prenatal and infant death rates for boys are higher.
- Up to the age of 10, girls are generally healthier than boys; they have fewer illnesses and require fewer doctor visits.
- Girls usually start their pre-teen growth spurt on an average of two years before boys. Around the age of 12, girls are usually taller and heavier than boys.
- At all ages, males have narrower pelvic outlets, broader shoulders, and a lower fat-to-muscle ratio than females.
- Because of their lower amount of body fat, boys have less ability to float in water or to withstand the cold than girls.
- From early childhood, boys display a higher level of aggressive behavior than girls. This is true in most cultures and in most animal species.
- The life span of females is an average of seven years longer than that of males.

- Females are more sensitive to taste, smell, touch, and high tones than males.
- Males after the age of 8 have somewhat better visual-spatial abilities that is, seeing objects or figures in space and how they are related.

BODY TRAPS

Being female has never been easy, especially when one considers the traps and tortures inflicted on girls and women for the sake of beauty. History and the study of many cultures shows an obsessive preoccupation with female bodies. In recent times, the Barbie doll look has given girls an unachievable image of the female body. In fact, Barbie translated into real female flesh would result in a woman whose feet were so small she couldn't stand up, much less walk, and her waist would be a good 10 inches smaller than any real female's. Let's look at some of the life-threatening ways girls and women reshaped themselves to look like Barbie or some other beauty equivalent.

Feet
In China, beginning in the eleventh century, the practice of foot binding was used on female infants. The feet were tightly bound to prevent growth. The toes dropped off and a deep cleft formed between the heel and the front of the foot. Small feet were a sign of beauty and class. Binding was done to distinguish large-footed working women from wealthy women of leisure. Women with bound feet were confined to the house because walking was so painful. This practice was forbidden by decree in the twentieth century.

The French painter Degas was fascinated by piquant de laideur, or the spice of ugliness, in girls and women he painted.

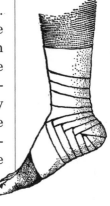

19

In America in the 1950s some women had their little toes surgically removed in order to wear high-heeled spiked shoes with severely pointed fronts.

Legs

In very recent times in America, some well-nourished girls who were growing taller than men were given growth-arresting treatments to keep them small and dainty. Other "too-tall" girls had bone sections surgically removed from their legs.

Waists

In the late 1800s some women had their two lower ribs surgically removed in order to achieve a small waist.

Breasts

In the 1960s some American women had liquid silicone injections to enlarge their breasts. This dangerous procedure often backfired. The silicone would solidify and travel through the body, causing infection, gangrene, and odd lumps in unusual places.

Today, some girls and women have breast augmentation surgery. A silicone pouch is implanted beneath the breast to push it outward.

Necks

Among the Padaung women of Burma, long necks are signs of beauty. Young girls wear brass or iron rings around their necks in order to stretch them. Beginning with five, the number of rings increases to a total of twenty-two in adulthood. The neck vertebrae are pulled apart and the rings can never be removed at the risk of death. These "beautiful"

necks are stretched to lengths of fourteen inches.

Teeth
Among the ancient Mayans of Mexico, girls and women filed their teeth into points and inlaid the teeth with jewels to enhance beauty.

Lips
In Africa, girls of the Sras Djunge begin to stretch their lips by implanting wooden disks at the age of 4. As the girls grow, the disks get larger and the lips stretch further until they are barely able to talk and can consume only liquids.

Today in America women have their lips surgically "plumped" with injections of silicone.

Faces
Cosmetic surgery in the United States is a big business. Of those who have surgery to correct minor flaws or make themselves more beautiful, 87% are girls and women. Some of the operations are: rhinoplasty, to reduce or reshape a nose; bepharoplasty, to remove eye wrinkles and bags; submandibular lipectomy, to "correct" a flabby chin; chemosurgery, to burn away upper skin layers and remove wrinkles; and face lifts, to tighten or remove sagging facial skin (the skin is stitched at the hairline to hide the scars).

Body weight
In the 1970s, American women who worried about their weight began to undergo bypass surgery to have their intestines sealed off to help them lose weight. Ninety percent of all the people who had this surgery were women. Also in the early '70s

Five of the contestants in the 1989 Miss America Pageant had had their breasts surgically reconstructed and enlarged.

women had their jaws wired together to prevent them from eating. In 1976 a surgical procedure known as stomach stapling was introduced. Women reduced the size of their stomachs by having fat removed and the stomach sutured back together. Liposuction, a surgical procedure in which body tissue is sucked out of the belly, is also done. Some women think that these procedures will help them lose weight, but the fact is that they are dangerous and the results don't last.

Anorexia and bulimia

At one time in history, teenage girls starved themselves in rebellion against an arranged marriage or as a sacrifice to a god or a saint. Today, American girls and women starve themselves in the name of beauty. Anorexia nervosa is a compulsive fear of and fixation upon food. Thousands of American females die of anorexia each year. They simply starve themselves to death.

Bulimia is an eating disorder in which a person eats but later regurgitates the food. This is a way of tasting and eating but purging oneself of the calories and fat, another way of starving oneself.

FOOD FOR THOUGHT
- Fat was once called the "silken layer."
- You don't have much control of your body if you can't eat.
- Fat means fertility. Female fat is not in itself unhealthy.
- Ultra-skinny models, actresses, and dancers weigh 23% less than the average American woman.

- Before 1920 soft rounded hips, thighs, and bellies were considered attractive and desirable.
- Cellulite (dimpled fat) is normal flesh. Fashion magazines have labeled it unsightly.
- Recently a reader to a teen magazine wrote asking, "Why is it that fat on our thighs is considered grotesque, yet put the same fat on our breasts and it is considered sexy?"

BEAUTY CONTESTS

What is beauty and what are beauty contests about? If "beauty is in the eye of the beholder," what are the beholders saying about beauty in competition? Let's check out a few facts about beauty pageants around the world:

- In Nigeria, the Wodaabe tribe hold beauty contests for men. The women in the tribe hold all the economic power. The men spend hours in elaborate makeup sessions, then they compete in beauty contests judged by the women.
- When foot binding was common in China, the Chinese held tiny foot festivals. The women stood behind curtains with only their feet showing. Their beauty was judged by the size of their feet.
- The largest single beauty contest in the world is the Miss Hemisphere Pageant. Girls as young as 3 years old are judged on beauty, charm, poise, and personality. In this competition toddlers wear false eyelashes and tasseled bikinis.
- The Miss America Pageant began as a bathing beauty contest to attract tourists to Atlantic City, New Jersey. Today it is called a scholarship program, but nothing has changed. The scholarship winners still have to look good in a bathing suit.

"Prettiness can masquerade as beauty for a moment until it stales, for prettiness is true beauty's enemy."
—Hyatt Mayor, curator of Metropolitan Museum of Art

BODY BEAT

Here are a few good tips on how to care for your body with natural, effective, and inexpensive remedies.

Cold feet?

Sprinkle ground cayenne pepper into your socks. It will warm your feet without burning.

Sweet relief

A 4,000-year-old remedy for minor cuts, scrapes, and burns is sugar. Use a paste of white granulated sugar and water on nonbleeding cuts. The sugar cleanses, speeds healing, and reduces scarring.

Chicle your teeth

When you can't brush or floss your teeth after a meal, try chewing sugarless gum. Wait five minutes after the meal and don't chew for more than fifteen minutes. The gum chewing stimulates saliva secretion, which squeezes between teeth and zaps tooth decay acids.

Blemish blaster

Gently massage a paste of baking soda and warm water over blemished areas. The baking soda absorbs oils and helps maintain the skin's pH balance. Rinse with water. Apply hydrogen peroxide (3%) with a cotton ball. Hydrogen peroxide is a disinfectant which will turn blackheads white.

Milky mask

Apply milk of magnesia in layers over your face if you have problems with oily skin. Let it dry for fifteen minutes, then rinse thoroughly. The liquid magnesium absorbs oil and disinfects.

FEELING GOOD

Your body and your mind are totally connected. Here are some of the things you can do with your body and mind to feel good about yourself. These suggestions came from other girls in the United States.

- Put on comfortable clothes, clothes that make you feel unselfconscious, and go out for a walk. Walking clears your head so you can collect your thoughts and enjoy your surroundings.

- Take one afternoon from your busy schedule and zone out. Either snooze, read a book, or play a game with friends.

- Take a warm, soothing, herbal bath (like Marie Antoinette used to do): combine bay leaves, thyme, and marjoram, and tie them into a washcloth. Throw it into the running bath water with a cup of salt. Relax.

- Keep a diary, in a journal or on a tape recorder, and make entries at least twice a week. Don't hold back. Keep track of how you feel.

- Listen to your favorite music.

- Paint a mural or a self-portrait. Use your imagination.

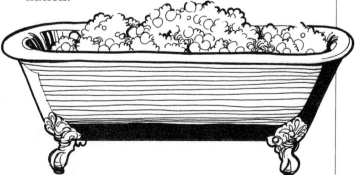

- Keep a journal of your dreams.

- Have fun with your hair. Lots of girls like to use hennas or rinses with a bright, Kool-Aid color. These colorings aren't permanent and won't hurt your hair.

- Try to relax all the muscles in your body by first tensing them and then letting them go. Work from your toes on up to your head.

- Yoga and stretching are great stress reducers and body toners. Yoga promotes strength, balance, flexibility, good posture, and a sense of well-being.

- To take your mind off problems, find a quiet spot, close your eyes, relax your body, and picture yourself in perfectly peaceful or dreamy surroundings. This is a form of meditation.

- When you are stressed or emotionally jammed up, close your eyes and take three very deep breaths, each time exhaling completely till most of the air is out of your lungs. This will refresh you and help you think more clearly.

- Turn on the music and dance. You can twirl by yourself or find a broom to waltz with.

- Express your anger—it's healthy. If you don't like something, say so, and then try to change it. If you can't change it, at least change the way you think about it.

Do you have tips for feeling good that you'd like to share? Write us a letter!

GOOD-FOR-YOUR-BODY FOODS

According to folklore, the following foods are good for you. Now scientists agree.

- Cranberry juice is good for urinary tract infections. Why? Because the juice inhibits a bacteria that clings to the wall of the bladder and causes infection.

- Carrots are good for your eyes. Carrots and some other fruits and vegetables contain beta carotene, which can reduce the chance of eye disease. One carrot a day can help prevent macular degeneration, which eventually leads to blindness.

- Chicken soup fights congestion that comes with a cold. Chicken has an amino acid that thins the mucous lining of the sinuses, thus relieving stuffiness.

- Garlic and onions kill flu and cold viruses.

- Fish is good for your brain. The mineral zinc is found in fish and shellfish. Studies show that even a minimal deficiency of zinc impairs thinking and memory.

- Blueberries fight the bacteria that causes diarrhea.

- Bananas are a natural antacid. They soothe heartburn or gastric distress.

- Spinach is good for your spirits. It contains lots of folic acid. If your body doesn't have enough folic acid, you may feel depressed.

- Ginger root fights nausea caused by motion sickness and relieves migraine headaches. Make a tea of fresh ginger root by simmering it in water for ten minutes.

- Eat onions to fight insomnia. Onions contain a mild natural sedative called quercetin.

- Yogurt with acidophilus fights the bacteria that causes vaginal yeast infections.

SEXUAL HARASSMENT

What's the difference between flirting and sexual harassment? Flirting can be fun, you take a willing part in it, and it's playful and harmless. Sexual harassment is not fun. It may take the form of an unwanted or lewd remark, a note with sexual content, or actual grabbing of a girl's body or pulling down her pants, sometimes just "for fun." It isn't always initiated by a man and directed at a woman, either, even though women are usually the targets of this kind of abuse. It can make girls and women feel violated, depressed, inferior, and scared. Sexual harassment in its many forms has become widespread, especially in American schools. Here are some tips on what you should do if you feel you are the target of sexual harassment.

1. Don't ignore it—that won't make it go away. If you feel uncomfortable or scared, tell someone.

2. Keep a written record of any incident. Include names of witnesses if there are any. Save any notes that are sexually explicit.

3. Tell the person to stop. With the help of a trustworthy adult, write a letter describing the harassment and demanding that it stop and deliver it to the harasser. Save a copy of your letter.

4. Never blame yourself for the harassment. Remember that you are not trapped or helpless. Your parents and school officials can help you.

5. Notify a guidance counselor, teacher, or principal who will believe you and will do something. If all else fails, send a letter to your state's department of education describing what happened.

In a 1992 survey of girls in grades 2 through 12, 89% of the respondents said they had been targets of unwanted sexual gestures, looks, or comments.

Calendar

Women's

Words,

Celebrations,

Birthdays,

and Firsts

JANUARY

1 Betsy Ross was born Elizabeth Griscom on this day in 1752. She is said to be the maker of the first U.S. flag.

2 Today is Z Day. In recognition of all girls whose names begin with Z.

3 Lucretia Coffin Mott was born on this day in 1793. She was a famous Quaker minister who fought for the rights of slaves and women.

4 Elizabeth Ann Seton died on this day in 1821. She was the first American to be named a saint by the Roman Catholic Church. She founded a Catholic elementary school and laid the foundation for the U.S. parochial school system.

5 Nellie Tayloe Ross became the first female state governor on this day in 1925. She governed the state of Wyoming.

6 Joan of Arc, the French soldier, visionary, and saint, was born on this day in 1412.

7 Zora Neale Hurston, author and folklorist, was born on this day in 1891.

8 Today is Women and Midwives Day in Greece. It is a day to honor Greek women, who have the day off from housework and childcare.

9 Carrie Chapman Catt was born on this day in 1859. She was the founder of the League of Women Voters. Catt was, together with Susan B. Anthony, most responsible for winning the right to vote for American women.

10 Coco (Gabrielle) Chanel died on this day in 1971. She was a French clothing designer who invented the concept of sportswear, banned the corset and ruffly petticoats, and created Chanel No. 5 perfume, still the bestseller of all scents.

11 Alice Paul was born on this day in 1885. She authored the original draft of the Equal Rights Amendment and founded the National Woman's Party.

FLOWER:
Snowdrop
STONE:
Garnet

12 After her husband's death in 1931, Hattie Wyatt Caraway was appointed to complete his Senate term. On this day in 1932 she became the first woman elected to the U.S. Senate, serving as senator from Arkansas.

13 Charlotte Ray was born on this day in 1850. She became the first African American woman lawyer in the U.S.

14 Faye Dunaway, actor, was born in Florida on this day in 1941. She was nominated for an Oscar for her first movie, *Bonnie and Clyde,* and won an Oscar in 1976 for her role in *Network.*

15 *Korean Festival of the Five Grains.* This is a celebration of female fertility.

16 On this day in 1978 the first women U.S. astronaut were selected. They were: Anna Fisher, Shannon Lucid, Judith Resnick, Sally Ride, Margaret Seddon, and Kathryn Sullivan.

17 Martha Cotera, a Chicana feminist, librarian, and civil rights worker, was born on this day in 1938.

18 The first woman to walk to the North Pole was 30-year-old Ann Bancroft of St. Paul, Minnesota. Along with the seven other members of the expedition, she set out from Ward Hunt Island in Canada. They traveled 1,000 miles in 55 days and reached the North Pole on this day in 1986.

19 On this day in 1977, Iva D'Aquino, also known as Tokyo Rose, was pardoned by U.S. President Gerald Ford for crimes of treason during World War II.

20 Ruth St. Denis was born on this day in 1879. She was an American dancer and choreographer best known for *Radha,* her dance about a Hindu goddess. She cofounded with her husband, Ted Shawn, the Denishawn Dance School and Dance Company in Los Angeles.

21 On this day in 1993, the first research center in the U.S. to study girls in sports opened at the University of Minnesota.

22 *Roe v. Wade Decision Day.* On this day in 1973, women in the U.S. won the right to privacy (which included the right to have an abortion) by a decision of the U.S. Supreme Court in the famous case of *Roe v. Wade.*

23 Elizabeth Blackwell, the first woman doctor in the U.S., graduated first in her class on this day in 1849. Twenty thousand people watched her receive her degree from Geneva College in New York.

24 The prima ballerina Maria Tallchief was born on this day in 1925 on an Oklahoma Indian reservation. Later she co-founded with her husband, George Balanchine, the New York City Ballet.

25 Elizabeth Cochrane Seaman, who used the pen name Nellie Bly, completed her trip around the world on this day in 1890. She was a New York journalist who took up the challenge to travel around the world in less than 80 days. Her world record time was 72 days, 6 hours, 11 minutes.

26 Constance M.K. Applebee died on this day in 1981 at the age of 107. Born in England, she was responsible for introducing field hockey to the U.S. in 1901.

27 Ah-yoka, the 12-year-old daughter of Sequoyah, a Cherokee scholar, was the first person to learn to read the written Cherokee language.

28 On this day in 1986, the space shuttle *Challenger* exploded in midair. Aboard were two women: the astronaut Judith Resnick and Christa McAuliffe, a teacher and the first civilian woman in space.

29 Oprah Winfrey, actor and talk show host, was born on this day in 1954.

30 Margaret Donahue died on this day in 1978. She was the first woman executive in baseball when she became vice president of the Chicago Cubs in 1950.

31 Anna Pavlova was born on this day in 1881. She was a Russian prima ballerina known for roles in *Coppelia, Giselle,* and *Swan Lake.* The part of the dying swan in *Swan Lake* was created for her.

FEBRUARY

1 On this day in 1978 a postage stamp honoring Harriet Tubman was issued. She was the first African American woman to have her likeness on a U.S. postage stamp.

2 Christie Brinkley was born on this day in 1953.

3 Gertrude Stein was born on this day in 1874. She was an American writer of fiction, poetry, and plays. She is well known for her words, "A rose is a rose is a rose."

4 Betty Friedan, feminist leader and writer, was born on this day in 1921.

FLOWER:
Violet
GEM:
Amethyst

5 Marianne Moore died on this day in 1972. She was an American poet best known for translating fairy tales and for her collections of poetry, including "O To Be Dragon."

6 Today is Midwinter Day in the Northern Hemisphere. In the Southern Hemisphere, summer is half over.

7 Laura Ingalls Wilder was born on this day in 1867. She was the author of a series of autobiographical novels known as the Little House books.

8 On this day in 1587, Mary Queen of Scots was beheaded at the age of 44. She was convicted of plotting to overthrow her cousin, Elizabeth I, queen of England.

9 Alice Walker, essayist, poet, and novelist, was born on this day in 1944. She won the Pulitzer Prize in 1983 for her novel *The Color Purple*.

10 Leontyne Price, operatic soprano, was born on this day in 1927.

11 Jane Yolen was born on this day in 1939. She is the author of many children's books, among them, *Owl Moon*.

12 Judy Blume was born on this day in 1938. She is the popular author of young adult realistic fiction, including *Iggy's*

House, Just As Long As We're Together, and *Are You There God? It's Me, Margaret.*

13 Today is Get a Different Name Day. If you dislike or find your own name boring, take a new one today.

14 Anna Howard Shaw was born on this day in 1847. She was the first woman to be ordained a minister in the Methodist Church.

15 Susan Brownell Anthony was born on this day in 1820. She fought for equal voting rights, equal pay, and equal marital rights for women. She was the first American woman to appear on a coin, the Susan B. Anthony dollar.

16 Leonora O'Reilly was born on this day in 1870. She was a union leader and one of the founders of the NAACP, the National Association for the Advancement of Color People.

17 The PTA was founded on this day in 1897 by Phoebe Hearst and Alice McLellan.

18 Mary I, Queen of England, was born in 1516. She attempted to replace the state religion of Protestantism with Catholicism. For this cause more than 300 people were burned at the stake. She became known as Bloody Mary.

19 Carson McCullers, author, was born on this day in 1917. She dramatized her novel, *The Member of the Wedding,* and it became a long-running Broadway hit.

20 Angelina Grimké was born in 1805. She and her sister, Sarah, were among the first American women to speak to audiences of both men and women. They fought against slavery and for women's rights.

21 Erma Bombeck, humorist, columnist, and author, was born on this day in 1927. Her books include *If Life Is a Bowl of Cherries, What Am I Doing in the Pits?* and *When You Look Like Your Passport Picture, It's Time to Go Home.*

22 Drew Barrymore, actor, was born on this day in 1975.

23 Ruth Nichols was born on this day in 1901. She was a pioneer aviator who set many records for speed and altitude. In 1930 she was the first woman to fly cross-country, which she did in 13 hours, 21 minutes—one hour less than Charles Lindbergh.

24
> *Be an outcast:*
> > *Be pleased to walk alone*
> > > *(Uncool)*

from "Be Nobody's Darling," from *Revolutionary Petunias and Other Poems* by Alice Walker

25 Adele Davis was born on this day in 1905. She was a writer on nutrition who promoted taking vitamins and eating natural foods for good health. Her message was "You are what you eat."

26 Today is Blue Jean Day. They have been around for more than 100 years. Wear a pair today to commemorate the birth of their creator, Levi Strauss.

27 Elizabeth Taylor was born on this day in 1932. She was the child star of *National Velvet* and appeared in numerous other movies. She has been a major spokesperson in the fight against AIDS.

28 Mary Lyon was born on this day in 1797. She founded Mount Holyoke College, a prominent women's college in Massachusetts.

29 Today is Leap Year Day. This day occurs once every four years when the extra hours of the solar year add up to another day.

MARCH

1 Robyn Smith was the first woman jockey to win prize money when she rode the horse North Sea to victory at Aqueduct Raceway in New York in 1973.

2 The first women's hotel, The Barbizon, opened in New York City on this day in 1878.

3 Today is Girls' Doll Day in Japan. *Hinamatsuri* is a national festival during which families bring out dolls handed down through generations. The dolls are likenesses of Japan's empresses and emperors. Girls learn about the history and culture of their country through these dolls.

4 The zoologist Jane Goodall was born on this day in 1934 in London, England. In the 1960s and 1970s she began her life's work, living among and studying chimpanzees on the shores of Lake Tanganyika in Africa. In 1971 she published her popular work on chimps, *In the Shadow of Man*.

5 Louise Pearce was born on this day in 1885. She was a scientist who developed a drug to control sleeping sickness.

6 Anna Claypoole Peale was born on this day in 1791. She came from a family of American painters and is thought to be the first female professional portrait painter in the U.S.

7 In Wyoming in 1870, for the first time in U.S. history, women were allowed to serve on a grand jury.

8 *International Women's Day*. A day to honor the world's working women. First proclaimed in 1910, it commemorated a protest by female garment workers in New York City in 1857.

9 This is National Panic Day. Everyone is allowed to panic today!

10 *Harriet Tubman Day*. She founded the Underground Railroad, which helped more than 300 slaves reach freedom in the northern states. She was a nurse, spy, and scout during the Civil War. Later she worked for the rights of women and the elderly. She died on this day in 1913.

FLOWER:
Daffodil

GEM:
Aquamarine

11 Children's book author Wanda Gag was born on this day in 1893. Her most famous book is *Millions of Cats*.

12 Today is Girl Scout Day. The Girl Scouts of America was founded in 1912 by Juliette Gordon Low. The first scout was Margaret (Daisy) Gordon, her niece.

13 Abigail Powers Fillmore was born on this day in 1798. As First Lady, she established the White House library.

14 Lucy Hobbs Taylor was born on this day in 1833. She was the first woman in the U.S. to become a dentist (in 1866). She taught her husband about dentistry, and he too became a dentist.

15 Margaret Webster was born on this day in 1905. She was the first woman stage director at the Metropolitan Opera House in New York City.

16 Sarah Caldwell was born on this day in 1924. An opera producer and director, she was the first woman to conduct at the Metropolitan Opera House in New York City.

17 *St. Patrick's Day.* Famous Irish women include Bernadette Devlin, Sinead O'Connor, and Edna O'Brien.

18 On this day in 1926, women were first allowed to practice law in Turkey.

19 "True [female] emancipation begins neither at the polls nor in the courts. It begins in woman's soul."
—Emma Goldman, feminist, revolutionist.

20 Today is Harriet Beecher Stowe Day. On this day in 1852 her famous book *Uncle Tom's Cabin* was published. Its description of slavery's cruelty awakened the American conscience.

21 *International Astrology Day.* What's your sign?

22 The first women's college basketball game was played at Smith College in 1892. The organizer was Senda Berenson, known as the mother of basketball.

23 Today is Melba Toast Day. On this day in 1901 melba toast was created by and named for Dame Nellie Melba, an Australian opera singer.

---

24 Elizabeth I, Queen of England, died on this day in 1603. This ended her forty-five-year reign, which was called the Golden Age or the Elizabethan Age because of the great achievements in England during that time.

---

25 Aretha Franklin, the singer nicknamed the "Queen of Soul," was born on this day in 1942.

---

26 Sandra Day O'Connor born on this day in 1930. She was the first woman Supreme Court Justice.

---

27 Happy birthday, Patti Hill! Born on this day in 1868, she is famous for writing the words to the song "Happy Birthday to You."

---

28 The Seven Sister Colleges are: Barnard, Mount Holyoke, Radcliffe, Smith, Vassar, Bryn Mawr, and Wellesley.

---

29 In 1994, 11-year-old Anna Paquin won the Oscar for best supporting actress for her role in the movie *The Piano*. She had never acted before.

---

30 On this day in 1886 Dorothy Eustis, founder of the Seeing Eye school, was born.

---

31 In a letter written on this day in 1776, Abigail Adams asked her husband John, a member of the Continental Congress, to "Remember the Ladies and be more generous and favorable than your ancestors were."

APRIL

1 *April Fools' Day*

2 *International Children's Book Day.* This day was designated to promote understanding through literature among the world's young people.

3 The 66-year-old Brownie uniform was radically updated on this day in 1993. The once all-brown dress was changed to floral-print vests, pastel-colored tops, and culotte jumpers, and released with the announcement by Girl Scout officials that "Not all kids like brown."

4 Dorothea Lynde Dix was born on this day in 1802. She was a crusader for the humane treatment of the mentally ill.

5 Sybil Luddington was born on this day in 1761. She was a Revolutionary War hero who, at the age of 16, rode 40 miles at night to get reinforcements for the Americans.

6 Today is No Housework Day. "The most wasteful 'brain drain' in America today is the drain in the kitchen sink." —Elizabeth Gould Davis, *The First Sex* (1971)

7 The National Museum of Women in the Arts opened in Washington, D.C. on this day in 1987.

8 Mary Pickford was born on this day in 1893. She was an Academy Award–winning actress who helped found the United Artists Corporation.

9 Florence Price, the first female African American symphonic composer, was born on this day in 1888.

10 Frances Perkins was born on this day in 1880. She became the first woman appointed to a U.S. presidential cabinet when Franklin D. Roosevelt named her Secretary of Labor.

11 On this day in 1953, Oveta Culp Hobby became the first woman to serve as Secretary of Health, Education, and Welfare. She was also the first director of the Women's Army

FLOWER:
Sweet Pea
GEM:
Diamond

Auxiliary Corps (WAAC), and the first woman to receive the U.S. Army Distinguished Service Medal.

12 Beverly Cleary was born on this day in 1916. She is best known for her series of books about Ramona Quimby and Henry Huggins.

13 Anne Sullivan was born on this day in 1866. She became famous as the teacher of Helen Keller, who was blind and deaf. The movie *The Miracle Worker* tells the story of these women's lives.

14 Loretta Lynn was born on this day in 1935. She is a country music singer and songwriter.

15 Bessie Smith, blues and jazz singer, was born on this day in 1894. She was the most successful black recording artist and performer of her time. She is known as the "Empress of the Blues."

16 Marie Gresholtz Tussaud died on this day in 1850. She was a Swiss wax modeler and was highly skilled by the time she was 17. The historical figures she represented can be seen in Madame Tussaud's Wax Museum in London, England.

17 Sirimavo Bandaranaike was born in Ceylon in 1916. She became the world's first woman prime minister (of Sri Lanka, formerly Ceylon) in 1960.

18 "I don't believe fine young ladies enjoy themselves a bit more than we do, in spite of our burnt hair, old gowns, one glove apiece, and tight slippers that sprain our ankles when we are silly enough to wear them." Jo speaking in *Little Women,* by Louisa May Alcott.

19 *Look-Alike Day.* This day recognizes people who look like someone famous.

20 Marie Curie and her husband discovered radium on this day in 1898.

21 Charlotte Brontë was born on this day in 1816. Her most famous novel is *Jane Eyre.* "*Jane Eyre* is one of the first female versions of the classic hero's journey from adolescence to maturity," wrote Gloria Steinem.

22 Today is Earth Day, a special day to honor Mother Earth.

23 Today is *Libra Dia*. This means Book Day in Spanish. On this day, the Spanish exchange their favorite books, much the way people in the U.S. exchange valentines.

24 American novelist Willa Cather died on this day in 1947. She was the first woman to win the Pulizer Prize for fiction with *One of Ours*. Her novels deal with life in the Nebraska of her youth.

25 Ella Fitzgerald was born on this day in 1918. She is well known for her style of scat singing and has an international reputation for singing blues, calypso, and Dixieland music.

26 Anita Loos was born on this day in 1893. She is famous for her novel *Gentlemen Prefer Blondes,* which has been turned into a play, a Broadway musical, and a film.

27 Today is Take Our Daughters to Work Day. This is a day devoted to girls' ideas and dreams. It is sponsored by the Ms. Foundation.

28 Mary Wollstonecraft, a British author, was born in April, 1759. Her book *Vindication of the Rights of Women* was the first to assert that women, like men, are human beings and should be treated equally.

29 On this day in 1925, Florence Sabin became the first woman elected to the National Academy of Sciences. She was also the first woman to graduate from Johns Hopkins Medical School. She studied the origin of blood cells.

30 Sarah Josephine Hale died on this day in 1879. She was the author of "Mary Had a Little Lamb."

MAY

1 Mary Harris Jones, known as Mother Jones, was born on this day in 1830. She organized American coal miners to strike for better working conditions and higher wages. She spent time in jail at the age of 70 on behalf of the workers.

2 On this day in 1970 Diane Crump became the first female jockey to ride in a Kentucky Derby.

3 The first national women's group to promote the interest of women in law was formed on this day in 1899. The first president of the Women Lawyers' Association was Edith Griswold, a patent lawyer.

4 The American actor and child advocate Audrey Hepburn was born on this day in 1929. She debuted on Broadway in *Gigi* and won an Oscar for her first movie, *Roman Holiday*.

5 *Cinco de Mayo Day.* A Mexican national holiday. Famous Mexican women include: Frida Kahlo, Laura Esquivel, and Juana Inés de la Cruz.

6 The first jazz festival for women musicians was held in Kansas City on this day in 1978. Marian McPartland, Betty Carter, and Toshiko Akiyoshi were among the performers.

7 Martha Washington hosted the first presidential inaugural ball on this day in 1789 in New York City.

8 Today is No Socks Day. The result will be less laundry, no searching for lost sock mates, and freer-feeling feet!

9 Candice Bergen was born on this day in 1946. She is an actor famous for her role as television's Murphy Brown.

10 Ella Grasso was born on this day in 1919. She was the first female elected governor in the U.S. She won the governorship of Connecticut in a landslide victory in 1974.

11 Martha Graham was born on this day in 1894. She was an American dancer and choreographer who pioneered modern dance.

FLOWER:
Lily of the valley
GEM:
Emerald

12 The English nurse Florence Nightingale was born on this day in Florence, Italy, in 1820. She was called the Lady with the Lamp because at night she carried a lamp through a hospital filled with wounded soldiers during the Crimean War (1854). That light is now a symbol of care for the sick and freedom for women to do their own work.

13 Maria Theresa was born on this day in 1717. She became the Empress of Austria at the age of 23. A wise and able ruler, she unified the Austro-Hungarian Empire. One of her sixteen children was Marie Antoinette, Queen of France.

14 Antioch College in Ohio became the first coeducational college in the U.S. on this day in 1852.

15 On this day in 1851, the first sorority was founded by sixteen women at Wesleyan College in Macon, Georgia. First named Adelphians, they eventually became Alpha Delta Pi.

16 Pop singer Janet Jackson was born on this day in 1966. Her recordings include "Control" and "That's the Way Love Goes."

FLORENCE NIGHTINGALE

17 Women made their debut as White House Honor Guards on this day in 1978 during a welcoming ceremony for Zambia's President Kaunda. Jimmy Carter was the U.S. president.

18 On this day in 1953, Jacqueline Cochran broke the sound barrier by flying an F-86 over Roger's Dry Lake, California, at the speed of 652.337 miles per hour. She was 46 years old. Eleven years later, she flew at a speed of 1,429.2 mph, more than twice the speed of sound.

19 Indira Ghandi was the first woman elected prime minister of India on this day in 1966. She was the first woman ever to rule a democracy, but was assassinated by two of her security guards in 1984.

20 Amelia Earhart began the first solo flight by a woman across the Atlantic Ocean on this day in 1932. She took a can of tomato juice and a thermos of soup for her 14 hour, 56 minute flight from New Foundland to Ireland.

21 The American Red Cross was founded by Clara Barton on this day in 1881. She worked for ten years to establish this foundation, which provides peacetime disaster relief as well as wartime relief.

22 Mary Cassatt, an American painter, was born on this day in 1884. When she was 19 she told her father she wanted to be a painter, to which he replied "I would almost rather see you dead." Among her best loved paintings is *Mother and Child*.

23 Margaret Wise Brown was born on this day in 1910. She is most famous for her beloved book, *Goodnight Moon*.

24 The American physician Helen Taussig was born on this day in 1898. She specialized in children's heart disease and developed lifesaving surgery for blue babies.

25 Today is National Tap Dance Day. One of the most famous tap dancers of all time was Ruby Keeler, who danced in a series of musicals and returned to Broadway at the age of 60 to dance in *No No Nanette*.

26 Astronaut Sally Ride was born on this day in 1951. She was the first American woman to travel in space.

27 The American poet Julia Ward Howe was born on this day in 1819. She wrote "Battle Hymn of the Republic," which begins with the words: "Mine eyes have seen the glory of the coming of the Lord."

28 The Dionne quintuplets were born in Canada on this day in 1934. These five girls were the first quints to live to adulthood. They were Marie, Emilie, Yvonne, Annette, and Cecile.

29 On this day in 1921 the American novelist Edith Wharton became the first woman to win a Pulitzer Prize for fiction. She won the award for her novel *The Age of Innocence*.

30 Today Joan of Arc Feast Day is celebrated in France. Joan of Arc led the French army against the invading English army in 1429. She was captured and burned at the stake in 1431.

31 Brooke Shields, actor, was born on this day in 1965.

1 Marilyn Monroe was born Norma Jean Baker on this day in 1926. Her movies include *Some Like It Hot, Bus Stop,* and *The Misfits.*

2 Martha Custis Washington was born on this day in 1731. She was America's first First Lady.

3 Sally Jane Priesand, the first woman rabbi in the U.S., was ordained on this day in 1972.

4 Catharine McCulloch was born on this day in 1862. In 1898 she became the first woman to argue a case before the Supreme Court.

FLOWER:
Rose
GEM:
Pearl

5 Today is International Mothers' Peace Day. It was established in 1872 by Julia Ward Howe, who said, "Those who nurture life on earth are of one mind in their opposition to those who would destroy it."

6 On this day in 1872 Susan B. Anthony was arrested and fined for voting in an election. (Women had not yet attained the right to vote in the U.S.)

7 Gwendolyn Brooks was born on this day in 1917. She was the first African American woman to win a Pulitzer Prize for poetry. She won the prize for her second volume of poetry, *Annie Allen,* in 1950. One of her most popular poems is "We Real Cool."

8 Today is American Heroine Day. This is a day to honor all brave women.

9 June is the traditional month of marriages and has been since early Roman times.

10 Bridget Bishop of Salem, Massachusetts, was the first of the Salem "witches" to be hanged, on this day in 1692.

11 Jeanette Rankin was born on this day in 1880. She was the first woman elected to Congress. She fought for women's right to vote and was an ardent pacifist who, at the age of 87, led a protest against the Vietnam War (The Jeanette Rankin Brigade).

12 Today is Anne Frank's birthday. She was born in 1929 and is remembered for the diary she wrote while in hiding from the Nazis in Amsterdam during World War II.

13 *Children's Day*—A day to celebrate children worldwide.

14 Tennis champion Steffi Graf was born in Germany on this day in 1969. She won the Grand Slam in tennis in 1988— the Australian Open, French Open, Wimbledon, and U.S. Open titles. She became a professional player at the age of 13.

15 Today is Smile Power Day.

16 Mary Goddard was born on this day in 1738. She was the publisher of three colonial newspapers, was the first to print the Declaration of Independence with the names of the signers, and was the first woman to serve as a postmaster in the U.S.

17 The first Omaha Indian doctor, Susan La Flesche Picotte, was born on this day in 1865.

18 Today is American Woman Astronaut Day. On this day in 1983, Sally Ride began a six-day mission aboard the space shuttle *Challenger*.

19 On this day in 1984 Geraldine Ferraro, a Congresswoman from Queens, New York, became the first woman nominated by a major political party as candidate for vice president.

20 Victoria became queen of England on this day in 1837. She reigned for 64 years. The Victorian age in English history was named for her.

21 Today is Summer Solstice Day. This is the first day of summer and the longest day of the year in the Northern Hemisphere.

22 The American author Anne Morrow Lindbergh was born on this day in 1906. She is known for her book *A Gift from the Sea* and for her feats as an aviator. She once remarked, "Mothers and housewives are the only workers who do not have time off."

23 Wilma Rudolph was born on this day in 1940. She overcame severe physical disabilities to become a championship runner. In 1960 she became the first woman to win three gold medals at a single Olympics.

24 On this day in 1647 Margaret Brent appeared before the Maryland assembly demanding that women be given a voice and a vote. She was the first woman in Maryland to own property, and one of the first known suffragists in American history.

25 Rose Cecil O'Neill was born on this day in 1874. She was the New York author/illustrator who designed the Kewpie Doll. She made 1.5 million dollars from sales of her doll.

26 The American author Pearl Buck was born on this day in 1892. She spent her childhood in China with her missionary parents. A writer from girlhood, she wrote more than 100 books. In 1931 she won the Pulitzer Prize for *The Good Earth*. She became the first woman to win a Nobel Prize in literature (1935).

27 Emma Goldman was born on this day in Russia in 1869. An anarchist, she emigrated to the U.S. and lectured on free speech, women's rights, and birth control. She was the most uncompromising and courageous radical of her time.

28 Helen Keller, blind and deaf since infancy, graduated from Radcliffe College with honors on this day in 1904.

29 Elizabeth Dole was born on this day in 1936. She was a cabinet member in both the Reagan and Bush administrations. She left government in 1991 to serve as president of the American Red Cross.

30 On this day in 1936, Margaret Mitchell published her best-selling novel, *Gone with the Wind*. The story, set in the southern states during the Civil War, sold 50,000 copies in its first day in stores.

JULY

FLOWER:
Water lily
GEM:
Ruby

1 Nancy Lieberman was born on this day in 1958. She was the first woman to play in a men's professional basketball game.

2 The first U.S. coin picturing a woman was released on this day in 1979. Susan B. Anthony, advocate of women's rights, was selected for the one dollar coin. Unfortunately, the coin was too similar in size to the quarter and was not widely circulated.

3 Today marks the beginning of the dog days or hottest days of the year in the Northern Hemisphere. Ancient peoples sacrificed a brown dog on this day to appease the Dog Star, Sirius, who was believed to cause the hot weather.

4 Liza Redfield became the first woman to conduct an orchestra on Broadway on this day in 1960. She led a 24-piece orchestra in *The Music Man.*

5 Juanita Kreps became the first woman director of the New York Stock Exchange on this day in 1972. She later became the first woman appointed Secretary of Commerce.

6 Nancy Davis Reagan, the former First Lady, was born on this day in 1923. She popularized the slogan "Just Say No" in her national campaign against illegal drugs.

7 Mary Surratt was hanged on this day in 1865. She owned a boarding house where her son and John Wilkes Booth often met. John Wilkes Booth later assassinated President Abraham Lincoln. Surratt went to the gallows as a conspirator in Lincoln's assassination because she "kept the nest that hatched the egg."

8 On this day in 1911, Nan Jane Aspinwall arrived in New York City, completing a 4,500 mile solo horseback trip across the U.S.

9 Mathilde Krim was born on this day in 1926 in Italy. She became a world famous geneticist and philanthropist.

10 Mary McLeod Bethune was born on this day in 1875 on a plantation in South Carolina where she picked cotton all day and attended school between picking seasons. She went on to found a girls' school, the Bethune-Cookman College.

11 The American author Susan Warner was born on this day in 1819. She was the first novelist to sell one million copies of her book in the U.S. She wrote *The Wide, Wide World*.

12 Anne Moore was born on this day in 1871. She was an American librarian who is credited with starting storytelling hours in libraries.

13 Marcia Brown was born on this day in 1918. An American illustrator of children's books, she was the first to win the Caldecott Medal three times, for *Cinderella, or The Little Glass Slipper; Once a Mouse;* and *Shadow*.

14 American author Peggy Parish was born on this day in 1927. She is well loved for her series of Amelia Bedelia stories.

15 Frances Xavier Cabrini was born on this day in Italy in 1850. She emigrated to America in 1889 where she built a network of hospitals for the immigrant poor. She was canonized a saint in 1946.

16 Mary Baker Eddy was born on this day in 1821. She was a religious leader who founded the Christian Science movement. She also founded the daily newspaper the *Christian Science Monitor*.

17 Berenice Abbott was born on this day in 1898. She was a pioneer in American photography best remembered for her black and white photos of New York City.

18 Tenley Albright was born on this day in 1935. She was stricken with polio at the age of 11 but overcame her illness to become an Olympic gold medalist in figure skating. She went on to earn an M.D. from Harvard and became a surgeon.

19 The first U.S. women's rights convention was held on this day in 1848 in Seneca Falls, New York. Among other things the women proclaimed was, "We hold these truths to be self-evident: that all men and women are created equal."

20 Theda Bara was born on this day in 1890. She was the first female actor to wear eye makeup on screen. It was created for her by the designer Helena Rubinstein.

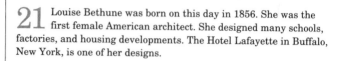

21 Louise Bethune was born on this day in 1856. She was the first female American architect. She designed many schools, factories, and housing developments. The Hotel Lafayette in Buffalo, New York, is one of her designs.

22 Emma Lazarus was born on this day in 1849. She wrote "The New Colossus," the poem that is inscribed on the Statue of Liberty. It expresses her faith in America as a haven for the poor and oppressed.

23 Harriet Strong was born on this day in 1844. She was an agriculturist and inventor who patented water storage dams.

24 Today is Amelia Earhart's birthday. She was a renowned American aviator who was born on this day in 1897.

25 Louise Brown, the first test tube baby, was born on this day in 1978 in Oldham, England. She weighed 5 pounds, 12 ounces.

26 Donaldina Cameron was born on this day in 1869. Working as a mission superintendent in San Francisco, she rescued over 2,000 Chinese girls and women from slavery.

27 The American figure skater Peggy Fleming was born on this day in 1948. At the age of 16, she was the youngest figure skater ever to win the National Championship. She also won the World Championship and a gold medal at the 1968 Winter Olympics.

28 Beatrix Potter was born on this day in 1866. She was the English author and illustrator who created the Peter Rabbit tales.

29 Lady Diana Spencer married Prince Charles, heir to the throne of England, on this day in 1981.

30 Anita Hill, law professor, was born on this day in 1956. In 1991 she testified nationally regarding the sexual harassment of women.

31 The last Playboy Club closed in the U.S. on this date in 1988.

AUGUST

1 Maria Mitchell was born on this day in 1818. She was the first American astronomer. In 1847 she discovered a comet which was later named Miss Mitchell's Comet. She was the first woman elected to the American Academy of Arts and Sciences.

2 The American figure skater Linda Fratianne was born on this day in 1960.

3 Maggie Kuhn was born on this day in 1906. She was an activist for rights of the elderly and founder of the Gray Panthers, a group that is dedicated to promoting a positive attitude toward aging.

4 On this day in 1944 the Nazis discovered Anne Frank's family's hiding place in Amsterdam. All the Franks died in concentration camps except Anne's father, who returned to the house and discovered her diary.

5 Ruth Sawyer was born on this day in 1880. She was a children's fiction writer who won the Newbery Medal in 1938 for her book, *Rollerskates*. She organized kindergartens in Cuba and worked as a storyteller in New York City.

6 On this day in 1926, American Gertrude Ederle became the first woman to swim across the English Channel. She was 20 years old when she accomplished the swim from Cap Gris-Nezly, France, to Dover, England, and beat the best man's record with a time of 14 hours and 13 minutes.

7 Mata Hari was born on this day in Amsterdam in 1876. Her real name was Margaretha Zelle. She was a belly dancer when she took the name Mata Hari, which means eye of the dawn. She was arrested and sentenced to death as a double agent who spied for both the French and the Germans in World War I.

8 Beatrice, Princess of York, was born in London on this day in 1988. Her mother is Sarah Ferguson, the Duchess of York; her father is Prince Andrew; and her grandmother is Queen Elizabeth.

9 Today is the International Day of Solidarity with the Struggle of Women in South Africa.

FLOWER:
Poppy
GEM:
Onyx

10 The American designer Betsey Johnson was born on this day in 1942.

11 On this day in 1862 American actor Sarah Bernhardt made her stage debut in Paris. She was 18 years old. Later known as the Divine Sarah, she has been called the most commanding personality in the history of modern Western theater.

12 In 1953, Anne Davidson became the first woman to sail alone across the Atlantic Ocean. She sailed from Plymouth, England, to Miami, Florida, in her 23-foot sloop, the *Felicity Anne.*

13 Annie Oakley was born on this day in 1860. She was a performer in Buffalo Bill's Wild West Show. She was a sharpshooter who could shoot her rifle and hit the edge of a playing card from more than 90 feet away.

14 Today is Middle Children's Day. This day is set aside to honor the kids born neither first, nor last, but in the middle. Emily Dickinson was a middle child; she had an older brother, Austin, and a younger sister, Lavinia.

15 The American author Edna Ferber was born in 1885. She wrote *Show Boat,* which was made into a musical, a play, and a movie. She won a Pulitzer Prize for *So Big,* a historical novel, in 1925.

16 Madonna, American singer and actor, was born on this day in 1958. Her full name is Madonna Louise Ciccone.

17 Charlotte Grimké was born on this day in 1837. She fought against slavery and became a teacher of freed slaves.

18 Virginia Dare was born in 1587. She was the first European baby born on American soil at Roanoke Island, Virginia.

19 The Daughters of the American Revolution was formed on this day in 1890. These women all trace their lineage to an ancestor who fought in the Revolution.

20 Connie Chung, journalist and national news anchorwoman, was born on this day in 1946 in Washington, D.C. Her birth name was Constance Yu-Hwa.

21 On this day in 1621, twelve young white women were sent from England to the colony of Virginia to be sold as slaves.

22 In 1762 Ann Franklin became the first woman editor of a U.S. newspaper. She worked for the *Mercury* in Newport, Rhode Island.

23 Today is Hug a Friend Day.

24 The American microbiologist Elizabeth Hazen was born on this day in 1885. In 1948 she discovered with Rachel Brown the antifungal antibiotic nystatin.

25 Ten-year-old Samantha Smith was killed in an airplane crash on this day in 1985. She was called "Maine's young ambassador of goodwill" after she was invited to Moscow to meet with Soviet leaders.

26 Women Get the Vote Day in the U.S. On this day in 1920, the nineteenth amendment to the U.S. Constitution was ratified, granting women the right to vote. It took 142 years for American women to win the privilege that American men of European descent had had since the Constitution was written.

27 Mother Teresa, Agnes Bojaxhiu, was born on this day in Yugoslavia in 1910. She devoted her life to helping the poor in the slums of India. In 1979 she received the Nobel Peace Prize.

28 Today is Dream Day, in honor of Martin Luther King's "I have a dream" speech.

29 Althea Gibson was the first African American woman to compete in the U.S. Open tournament on this day in 1950. She was also the first at Wimbledon in England in 1951.

30 On this day in 30 B.C., Cleopatra, queen of Egypt, died. She was the last ruler of the Macedonian Dynasty, which ruled Egypt from 323 B.C. to 31 B.C., when it was annexed to Rome.

31 Josephine Ruffin was born on this day in 1842. She was the president of the Woman's Era Club, the first black women's civic association.

SEPTEMBER

1 *Emma Nutt Day.* On this day in 1878 Emma Nutt of Boston, Massachusetts, was hired as the first female telephone operator in the U.S. She worked as an operator for 33 years.

2 Lydia Kamekeha Paki Liliuokalani was born on this day in 1838. She was the queen of Hawaii from 1891 to 1893.

3 Ann Richards was born on this day in 1933. This outspoken politician was elected governor of Texas in 1991.

4 This is the beginning of the hurricane season on the East Coast of the U.S. In 1953 only women's names were used to name hurricanes. The first one was Alice. Beginning in 1979, men's names were also used.

5 *Be Late for Something Day.*

6 Jane Addams was born on this day in 1860. She was the first American woman to win a Nobel Peace Prize. She was a social reformer who lived and worked among the poor and needy in the Hull House in Chicago. She willed her estate to the firstborn girl baby of each succeeding generation.

7 Anna Mary Moses, known as Grandma Moses, was born on this day in 1860. This American painter of rural life began painting when she was 76 years old. Between the ages of 100 and 101, when she died, she completed 25 paintings.

8 The first Miss America, 16-year-old Margaret Gorman from Washington, D.C., was crowned in 1921. At five feet one she was the shortest woman ever to hold the title. Years later, struggling through the Depression, she melted down her silver cup to pay her expenses.

9 Grace Kelly, American Academy Award–winning actor, later princess of Monaco, died on this day in 1982 in a car accident.

10 Demeter, the Greek goddess of agriculture, and Ceres, the Roman goddess of grain, the harvest, and agriculture (from whom the word cereal comes), are honored in this month.

FLOWER:
Morning glory
GEM:
Sapphire

11 Swedish singer Jenny Lind made her singing debut in America on this day in 1850. P.T. Barnum hired "the Swedish Nightingale" and paid her $1,000 per night plus profits to tour with his show. She was a shrewd businesswoman who earned $3 million a year at the peak of her career.

12 Azie Taylor Morton, the first African American woman treasurer of the U.S., took office on this day in 1977.

13 Maria Baldwin was born on this day in 1856. She was an educator and the first female African American principal of a school in Massachusetts (1889–1922).

14 Margaret Sanger was born on this day in 1879. She founded Planned Parenthood, an organization that promotes sex education and family planning.

15 The first women's professional club, Sorosis, was founded on this day in New York City in 1868. It was made up of journalists and career women who were not allowed to attend a Press Club Dinner for Charles Dickens.

16 The *Mayflower* left Plymouth, England, on this day in 1620. A baby girl, Oceania Hopkins, was born on board.

17 Maureen Connolly was born on this day in 1934. Nicknamed Little Mo, at 15 she was the youngest U.S. Girls' champion ever. She was also the first woman to win tennis's Grand Slam.

18 In 1881, Harriet Converse became the first white woman named as an honorary Native American chief. She was chief of the Six Nations and member of the secret Little Water Society. Her name was changed to Ya-ie-wa-noh, meaning She Who Watches Over Us.

19 In 1846 the English poet Elizabeth Barrett secretly left her father's house to marry the poet Robert Browning. Her father refused to ever see her again because he did not believe any of his children should marry.

20 Tennis player Billie Jean King won the "Battle of the Sexes" match on this day in 1973 by defeating Bobby Riggs in three straight sets of tennis at the Houston Astrodome.

21 Today is Biosphere Day. This is a day to remind all people of the fragility of Earth's atmosphere and the need to preserve it.

22 Today is American Businesswomen's Strut Day. This is a day in which thousands of businesswomen hit the streets at noon to raise scholarship money for girls and to honor the contributions of more than 53 million American career women.

23 Victoria Woodhull was born on this day in 1838. She was a feminist and the first woman candidate for the U.S. presidency, in 1872. Her running mate was Frederick Douglass, the black abolitionist leader.

24 Today is Native American Day. Some notable Native American women are Pocahontas, Sacajawea, Mourning Dove, and Wilma P. Mankiller.

25 Barbara Walters was born on this day in 1931. An American journalist and TV commentator, she was the first woman to co-anchor a daily evening news program. She was also the first woman in television to earn a million dollars a year.

26 "If I didn't start painting, I would have raised chickens." —Grandma Moses.

27 Mildred "Babe" Didrikson Zaharias died on this day in 1956. She was the most outstanding woman athlete of all time. She excelled in basketball, baseball, javelin throwing, track, and golf.

28 Kate Wiggin was born on this day in 1856. She organized the first free kindergarten in San Francisco and authored *Polly Oliver's Problem* and *Rebecca of Sunnybrook Farm*.

29 Caroline Yale was born on this day in 1848. She helped develop a popular system of teaching speech to the deaf.

30 Today is Chusok Day in Korea. This gala celebration honors the goddesses of crops.

OCTOBER

1 The world-class marathon runner Greta Waitz was born in Oslo, Norway, on this day in 1953.

2 Hannah Adams was born in 1775. She was the first woman professional writer in the U.S. Her book, *Alphabetical Compendium of Various Sects,* was an impartial history of various religions.

3 *National Book It! Day.* Sponsored by Pizza Hut, this is the largest reading incentive program in America. Seventeen million children take part in it every year.

4 Miriam Vanwaters was born on this day in 1887. She worked to reform conditions in women's prisons.

5 On this day in 1853, Rebecca Mann Pennell became the first female college professor at Antioch College in Ohio.

6 Shana Alexander, the American journalist, author, and television commentator, was born on this day in 1925.

7 On this day in 1975, women were first allowed to enter the U.S. military academies.

8 Mrs. O'Leary and her cow became famous on this day in 1871. Legend has it that the cow kicked over a lantern in the barn, starting the Great Chicago Fire.

9 It's World Post Day. Send a letter to a pen pal.

10 *Bonza Bottler Day.* Today we recognize the coinciding of the number of the day with the number of the month: 10–10.

11 Eleanor Roosevelt was born on this day in 1884. She was the first First Lady to become an advocate of human rights. She was an author and a diplomat.

12 Jean Nidetch was born in 1923. A compulsive eater in childhood, she weighed 214 pounds as an adult. With the help and encouragement of other heavy friends, she founded Weight Watchers in 1962.

FLOWER:
Calendula
GEM:
Opal

13 Mary Hays McCauley was born on this day in 1754. She became famous as "Molly Pitcher" when she fought in the Battle of Monmouth during the American Revolution in 1778.

14 Hannah Arendt was born on this day in 1906. A professor and political philosopher, she wrote on the moral responsibility of political action.

15 Helen Hunt Jackson was born on this day in 1830. In her book *A Century of Dishonor* she tells of the harrassment of Native Americans by the U.S. government. She challenged President Theodore Roosevelt to a debate on the plight of Indians.

16 Today is Dictionary Day. Check the dictionary for womanist words like *herstory* or *Ms.*

17 Today is Black Poetry Day. Gwendolyn Brooks, Maya Angelou, and Alice Walker are just a few of the poets whose verse you might read today.

18 Martina Navratilova was born on this day in 1956. She is a tennis great who won at Wimbledon nine times.

19 Annie Peck was born on this day in 1850. She was a classics scholar and a mountaineer. Beginning in 1895, she ascended mountains in Europe and South America dressed in knickerbockers, a tunic, and a felt hat tied by a veil. Her last climb was Mount Madison in New Hampshire at the age of 82.

20 Maud Nathan was born on this day in 1862. She was a woman suffragist and social worker and was thought to be the first woman in America to give a speech in a synagogue replacing a rabbi's sermon.

21 On this day in 1979, runner Greta Weitz became the first woman to run a marathon in less than 2.5 hours. It was the New York City marathon.

22 Harriet Chalmers was born on this day in 1875. She was the first woman outsider to travel to the inner regions of South and Central America (1900). She founded the Society of Women Geographers and wrote regularly for *National Geographic* magazine.

23 On this day in 1934, Jeanette Picard set an altitude record for women balloonists. She ascended 57,579 feet.

24 Annie Edson Taylor became the first person to go over Niagara Falls in a barrel on this day in 1901. She was a schoolteacher from Michigan who hoped this feat would make her rich. Unfortunately, her manager took most of the money and she died in 1921, penniless.

25 The first female FBI agents completed their training in 1972. Susan Lynn Roley and Joanne Pierce graduated from this 14-week course with 45 men.

26 Hillary Rodham Clinton was born on this day in 1947. She was the first First Lady lawyer and campaigned for national health care reform.

27 Maxine Hong Kingston was born on this day in 1940. Her autobiography, *The Woman Warrior,* describes the experience of being a Chinese-American female.

28 Happy birthday, Statue of Liberty! On this day in 1886, Liberty Enlightening the World was dedicated.

29 The National Organization for Women was founded on this day in 1966. Betty Friedan founded NOW to support "full equality for women in truly equal partnership with men."

30 Tonight is Mischief Night. The evening before Halloween is designated for kids to get an early start on harmless pranks.

31 Katherine Paterson was born on this Halloween day in 1932. In 1988 she won the Regina Medal for her lifetime contributions to children's literature. *Jacob Have I Loved* and *Bridge to Terabithia* are two of her novels.

FLOWER:

*Chrysan-
themum*

GEM:

Topaz

1   The first medical school for women opened on this day in 1848. It was named the Boston Female Medical School.

2   When poet Adrienne Rich won the 1974 National Book Award for *Diving into the Wreck,* she would not accept it alone, but shared the award with Alice Walker and Audre Lorde on behalf of all women.

3   Clara Noyes was born on this day in 1869. She was a teaching nurse who established the first hospital school for midwives in the U.S. in 1910.

4
November woods are bare and still;
November days are clear and bright;
Each noon burns up the morning's chill,
The morning's snow is gone by night.
—Helen Maria Fiske Hunt Jackson
(American poet, 1830–1885)

5   On this day in 1968, Shirley Chisholm of New York became the first African American congresswoman. Her motto was, "Unbought and unbossed."

6   After sailing solo around the world for 27 months, Tania Aebi, a 19-year-old American college student, returned to New York on this day in 1987. She was the first American woman and the youngest person ever to complete the journey alone.

7   Joni Mitchell was born on this day in Canada in 1943. Singer, songwriter, and painter, it was her song, "Chelsea Morning," that inspired First Daughter Chelsea Clinton's name.

8   Katharine Hepburn was born on this day in 1909. She is a legendary actress whose independence, strength, and sense of privacy have earned her the respect of millions.

9   Anne Sexton was born on this day in 1928. She was a Pulitzer Prize–winning poet whose works include *Live or Die.*

10   Today is National Young Readers Day. What's your favorite book? Recommend it to a friend today.

11 Abigail Adams was born on this day in 1744. She was a politically influential First Lady known for her letters, many of which were collected by her grandson and published.

12 Elizabeth Cady Stanton was born on this day in 1815. She was a writer and orator who demanded the vote for women. The mother of seven children, she is considered one of the founding mothers of American feminism.

13 Judianne Densen-Gerber was born in 1934. She was one of the founders of the National Center on Child Abuse and Neglect.

14 Astrid Lindgren was born in 1907. This Swedish author's gift to the world is the beloved character Pippi Longstocking.

15 Georgia O'Keeffe was born in 1887. This American painter left her mark on both American and twentieth-century art. She painted from the age of 12 to her death at age 99.

16 Esther Pohl Lovejoy was born on this day in 1869. She was the first woman physician to practice in the Klondike during the gold rush of the 1890s.

17 On this day in 1637, religious leader Anne Hutchinson was banished from the Massachusetts Bay Colony to the Long Island wilderness because she insisted to her Puritan brothers that women had the right to express themselves on church matters. She and her family, except one daughter, were killed by Indians.

18 Wilma Mankiller was born on this day in 1945. This Native American activist was the first woman to be elected chief of the Cherokee Nation of Oklahoma.

19 Jodie Foster was born in 1963. By the age of 13 she had established an acting career, but took time out to attend and graduate from Yale. She won her first Academy Award for best actress in 1988's *The Accused* and her second in 1991 for *The Silence of the Lambs*.

20 Pauli Murray was born on this day in 1910. A civil rights lawyer and Episcopal priest, she was the first African American to earn a doctorate from Yale Law School.

21 Phoebe Fairgrave Omilie was born on this day in 1902. She was an aerial stunt performer who was the first woman to obtain a federal pilot's license. She was also the first woman to earn an aircraft mechanic's license.

22 George Eliot, whose real name was Mary Ann Evans, was born on this day in 1819. An English novelist, she used a male pseudonym to publish her work and earned critical success for *Adam Bede, Mill on the Floss* and *Silas Marner*. One critic who praised her work wrote that novels by women are "inadequate and unreal" but this novel reached "the high standard of male genius."

23 Marie VanVorst was born on this day in 1867. She was an author and reformer who brought the poor working conditions of women factory workers to public attention.

24 In her memoirs, entitled *Hit,* published on this day in 1871, Dr. Mary Edwards Walker wrote, "You [men] are not our protectors....If you were, who would there be to protect us from?"

25 The singer Tina Turner was born in 1940. Her story was told in the movie *What's Love Got to Do with It.*

26 Mary Edwards Walker was born on this day in 1832. She was a Civil War surgeon who won the Congressional Medal of Honor.

27 Sarah Josepha Hale, an American magazine editor, persuaded Abraham Lincoln to proclaim Thanksgiving a national holiday.

28 Helen Magill White was born on this day in 1853. She was the first woman in the U.S. to earn a Ph.D., which she received from Boston University. She pursued postdoctoral studies in classics at Cambridge University in England in 1877.

29 Louisa May Alcott was born on this day in 1832. She is best remembered for her book *Little Women,* in which she created a strong heroine named Jo, the inspiration of many feminists.

30 In 1991 the U.S. soccer team became the first to win the Women's World Soccer Championship. The tournament was held in Guangzhov, China.

DECEMBER

1 Today is Rosa Parks Day. On this day in 1955, Rosa Parks, a middle-aged black woman, took a seat in the colored section of a bus in Montgomery, Alabama. When the bus became crowded, the bus driver told her to give up her seat to a white man. She refused and was arrested. Boycotts and protests followed and the Supreme Court decided to ban segregation on public transportation.

2 The actor Julie Harris was born in 1925. In thirty years of performing on Broadway, she has won five Tony Awards. She is best remembered for her one-woman show, *The Belle of Amherst* (1977), in which she played Emily Dickinson.

3 On this day in 1990, Mary Robinson was sworn in as the first woman president of Ireland.

4 *St. Barbara's Day.* According to legend, on this day a young woman places a twig from a cherry tree in a glass of water. If it blooms by Christmas Eve, she is certain to marry the following year.

FLOWER:
Poinsettia
GEM:
Turquoise

5 Elizabeth Agassiz was born on this day in 1822. She was an educator and the first president of Radcliffe College.

6 On this day in 1902, the first U.S. postage stamp picturing a woman was issued. Martha Washington appeared on a lilac-colored eight-cent stamp.

7 Willa Cather was born on this day in 1873. She was an American novelist who portrayed a series of independent women in her books. Her best-selling book was *Death Comes for the Archbishop.*

8 Mary Queen of Scots was born on this day in 1542. She became queen when she was six days old, at which time her mother also betrothed her to the French dauphin, Francis II.

9 Grace Hopper was born on this day in 1906. She was a Navy rear admiral and she developed the computer language known as COBOL.

10 Emily Dickinson was born on this day in 1830. She was an American poet who led a reclusive life. She wrote her poems on scraps of paper, sewed them in booklets, and hid them in trunks.

Only a dozen of her nearly 2,000 poems were published in her lifetime.

11 Annie Jump Cannon was born on this day in 1863. She was an astronomer who classified more than 350,000 stars.

12 Today is the Feast of Our Lady of Guadalupe Day. She is the patron saint of Mexico, and celebrations are held on this day in Mexico and parts of the southwestern U.S.

13 Today is St. Lucia Day in Sweden (Luciadagan). On this morning the eldest daughter of the family serves saffron-flavored buns and hot coffee to her parents before they rise from bed.

14 Margaret Chase Smith was born on this day in 1897. She was the first American woman to be elected to both houses of Congress. She was a congresswoman from 1940–1948 and a senator from 1948–1972.

15
They shut me up in Prose—
As when a little Girl
They put me in the Closet—
Because they liked me "still"
—Emily Dickinson

16 Margaret Mead was born on this day in 1901. She was an American anthropologist who wrote more than 30 books. Her fondest hope was to build one culture that "gives a place to every human gift."

17 Deborah Sampson was born on this day in 1760. She became a soldier in the American Revolution, disguising herself as a man named Robert Shurtleff in order to fight.

18 Gladys Henry Dick was born on this day in 1881. She was a microbiologist and physician who found the bacterial cause of scarlet fever.

19 Cicely Tyson, actor, was born on this day in 1939.

20 The first Broadway theater named for a living actress opened on this day in 1928. It was called The Ethel

Barrymore Theater. Ethel Barrymore debuted on stage at the age of 14 and won an Academy Award for *None But the Lonely Heart* at age 65.

21 Today is the Winter Solstice. This is the first day of winter in the Northern Hemisphere and the first day of summer in the Southern Hemisphere.

22 Aline Bernstein was born in 1880. She was a theatrical designer for many hit Broadway shows from 1920–1950.

23 Sarah Walker was born on this day in 1867. She was the first self-made American millionaire. She was an African American businesswoman who manufactured hair products as "Madam C. J. Walker."

24 Elizabeth Chandler was born in 1807. She was an author and abolitionist who boycotted goods produced by slaves.

25 Annie Lennox was born on this day in Scotland in 1954. She was the lead singer for the band Eurythmics, and went on to record songs like "Walking on Broken Glass" in her career as a solo artist.

26 Susan Butcher was born on this day in 1954. She has won the Iditarod several times; it is a 1,157-mile dogsled race.

27 Zona Gale, the first woman playwright to have a play produced on Broadway, opened her Pulitzer Prize–winning play, *Miss Lulu Bett,* on this day in 1920.

28 Carol Ryrie Brink was born on this day in 1895. She won the Newbery Medal for her book *Caddie Woodlawn,* which was inspired by her grandmother's stories of pioneer days in Wisconsin.

29 Mary Tyler Moore, actor and star of the popular TV series *The Mary Tyler Moore Show,* was born on this day in 1936.

30 Tracey Ullman, the English actor and singer, was born on this day in 1959.

31 *Make Up Your Mind Day.* Make a decision before the new year and follow through with it!

Crackerjack Kids and Careers

MOST OF US PLAY THROUGH our early years, struggle through our teen years, and wonder what we'll do  when we grow up. This should  be a decision we look forward to; in today's world, you can be anything you want to be.

FINDING A DIRECTION FOR LIFEWORK

- Make a list of all the things that interest you. Think about where you like to be, what you like to do, what kind of people you like to be with.

- List your strong points—your abilities, accomplishments, how you are valuable to others, and what you enjoy doing.

- List all your basic skills. Everyone is good at at least a few things. Here are some examples: reading, writing, cooking, selling things, performing, growing things, listening, teaching, solving problems, using tools, taking care of animals, making decisions, settling fights, painting, dressing creatively, building things, experimenting, working with numbers, making people laugh, etc.

- Next, put it all together and look at the following list of possibilities for a future career.

CAREERS TO CONSIDER

You can be anything you want to be. Here are only some of the careers that women have succeeded in:

Architects

Norma Sklarek was the first African American woman to earn a fellowship from the American Institute of Architects. She graduated from Columbia University's School of Architecture in 1950.

The American architect Eleanor Raymon established her own practice in 1928. She was constantly experimenting with new building materials and designed one of the earliest solar homes in 1948.

When she was young, Betty Saar, an accomplished artist, enjoyed searching for treasures in her grandmother's backyard. Little did she realize that this was the beginning of her career as a sculptor. Today Betty collects all kinds of objects to use in her compositions.

Natalie DeBlois was part of the team that designed Lever House in 1952, the Pepsi Cola building in 1959, and the Union Carbide building in 1960, all very large and famous corporate buildings.

When she was 21, Maya Lin won a national competition to design and build the now famous Vietnam Veterans Memorial in Washington, D.C. Her most recent monument was erected in Alabama in honor of the Civil Rights Movement.

Chefs
American-born Julia Child popularized French cooking in the United States with her television

show, *The French Chef,* in the 1960s. A graduate of the Cordon Bleu cooking school in Paris, her book, *Mastering the Art of French Cooking,* is considered the finest work on the subject.

M.F.K. Fisher (1908–1992) was an American chef and writer on the art of food. Her first book, *Serve It Forth,* was published in 1937. In it, she said "Look, if you have to eat to live, you might as well enjoy it." Good advice! Throughout the '40s, '50s, and '60s, she lived, cooked, and wrote in California, Switzerland, and France.

Alice Waters is a chef who came to fame when she opened her California restaurant Chez Panisse in 1971. Her latest cookbook was inspired by her 9-year-old daughter. It's called *Fanny at Chez Panisse* (1992) and is written in the voice of a young girl.

Philosophers

Hannah Arendt was a German-born philosopher (1906–1975). She lived most of her life in New York and wrote about the value of private over public virtues in her book *The Human Condition.*

The French philosopher Simone de Beauvoir became famous in 1949 when she published her book *The Second Sex.* In it she traced the oppression of women throughout history using her theories of psychology and myth.

Photographers

Berenice Abbot was born in the U.S. in 1898. After photographing famous people in Paris in the 1920s and in New York in the 1930s, she became a designer of technical photographic equipment.

Diane Arbus was an American photographer who became famous for her photos of extraordinary and sometimes bizarre people in the 1960s.

Margaret Bourke-White was a photojournalist whose World War II photos for *Life* magazine were world famous. She was the creator of the photo-essay, a series of photos that tell a story.

American Annie Leibovitz is a photographer of celebrities who has become a celebrity herself. At the age of 23 she became chief photographer for *Rolling Stone* magazine, where she worked from 1973 to 1983. She remains the best known photographer of her generation.

Publishers

Katharine Graham became the publisher of the *Washington Post,* one of the most influential and powerful newspapers in the U.S., in 1969. This newspaper is also the publisher of the weekly magazine *Newsweek*.

Victoria Ocampo of Argentina (1891–1979) was the founder and publisher of *Sur,* a literary magazine. She was known in her country as the Queen of Letters.

The American feminist, writer, editor, and speaker, Gloria Steinem, founded *Ms.* magazine in 1972.

Writers

There are many, many female writers alive today, and many more famous ones throughout history. Here are the prize winners:

NOBEL PRIZE WINNERS FOR LITERATURE

1909	Selma Lagerof of Sweden
1928	Sigrid Undset of Norway
1938	Pearl Buck of the U.S.
1945	Gabriela Mistral of Chile
1991	Nadine Gordimer of South Africa
1993	Toni Morrison of the U.S.

PULITZER PRIZE WINNERS FOR POETRY

1918	Sara Teasdale for *Love Songs*
1919	Margaret Widdemer for *Old Road to Paradise*
1923	Edna St. Vincent Millay for *The Ballad of the Harp-Weaver; A Few Figs from Thistles;* eight sonnets in *American Poetry, 1922, A Miscellany*
1926	Amy Lowell for *What's O'Clock*
1935	Audrey Wurdemann for *Bright Ambush*
1938	Marya Zaturenska for *Cold Morning Sky*
1952	Marianne Moore for *Collected Poems*
1956	Elizabeth Bishop for *Poems—North & South*
1961	Phyllis McGinley for *Times Three: Selected Verse from Three Decades*
1967	Anne Sexton for *Live or Die*
1982	Sylvia Plath for *The Collected Poems*
1984	Mary Oliver for *American Primitive*
1985	Carolyn Kizer for *Yin*
1987	Rita Dove for *Thomas and Beulah*
1991	Mona Van Duyn for *Near Changes*
1993	Louise Gluck for *The Wild Iris*

Pulitzer Prize–winning poet Rita Dove was named Poet Laureate of the U.S. in 1993.

PULITZER PRIZE WINNERS FOR FICTION

1921	Edith Wharton for *The Age of Innocence*
1923	Willa Cather for *One of Ours*
1924	Margaret Wilson for *The Able McLaughlins*
1925	Edna Ferber for *So Big*
1929	Julia Peterkin for *Scarlet Sister*
1931	Margaret Ayer Barnes for *Years of Grace*
1932	Pearl Buck for *The Good Earth*
1934	Caroline Miller for *Lamb in His Bosom*
1937	Margaret Mitchell for *Gone with the Wind*
1939	Marjorie Kinnan Rawlings for *The Yearling*
1942	Ellen Glasgow for *In This Our Life*
1961	Harper Lee for *To Kill a Mockingbird*
1965	Shirley Ann Grau for *The Keepers of the House*
1966	Katherine Anne Porter for *The Collected Stories of Katherine Anne Porter*
1970	Jean Stafford for *Collected Stories*
1973	Eudora Welty for *The Optimist's Daughter*
1983	Alice Walker for *The Color Purple*
1985	Alison Lurie for *Foreign Affairs*
1988	Toni Morrison for *Beloved*
1989	Anne Tyler for *Breathing Lessons*
1992	Jane Smiley for *A Thousand Acres*

PULITZER PRIZE WINNERS FOR DRAMA

1921	Zona Gale for *Miss Lulu Bett*
1931	Susan Glaspell for *Alison's House*
1935	Zoe Akins for *The Old Maid*
1945	Mary Chase for *Harvey*
1956	Frances Goodrich (with Albert Hackett) for *The Diary of Anne Frank*
1981	Beth Henley for *Crimes of the Heart*
1989	Wendy Wasserstein for *The Heidi Chronicles*

Here are more ideas for careers you could choose:

Accountant
Actor
Acupuncturist
Administrator
Airline pilot
Air traffic controller
Animal doctor or trainer
Announcer
Archaeologist
Architect
Art director
Artificial intelligence expert
Astrologer
Astronomer
Athlete
Attorney
Auctioneer
Audiologist
Auto mechanic
Bacteriologist
Baker
Banker
Biochemist
Bricklayer
Building contractor, inspector, manager
Calligrapher
Cartographer
Cartoonist
Chauffeur
Chef
Choreographer
Cinematographer
Clown
Comedy writer
Commodities trader

Communications technician
Computer graphics artist
Computer programmer
Conservationist
Conference planner
Corporate fitness director
Curator
Dentist
Design engineer
Detective
Dietitian/ nutritionist
Drama coach
Editor
Engineer
Engraver
Excavator
Exporter
Farmer
Fashion designer
Financial planner
Fish and game warden
Florist
Furniture designer
Gamekeeper
Gemologist
Geneticist
Geographer
Gerontologist
Historian
Horse trainer
Hospital administrator
Hypnotist
Illustrator

Instrument maker
Occupational therapist
Physician
Physical therapist
Psychologist
Psychometrist
Publisher
Radio producer
Recording engineer
Referee
Reporter
Reservations agent
Roboticist
Salesperson
Sample maker
Scrimshander
Science writer
Screenwriter
Seismologist
Set designer
Silversmith
Social worker
Sociologist
Sound mixer
Speech pathologist
Technical writer
Telemarketing representative
Teller
Tour operator
Translator
Travel agent
Underwriter
Urban planner
Volcanologist
Weather forecaster
Wildlife agent
X-ray technician

If you are wondering what career choices women have had in the past, take at look at these:

IN ANCIENT EGYPT

Midwife	Potter	Artist
Merchant	Temple Dancer	Poet
Weaver	Musician	Priestess

WOMEN'S WORK DURING THE STONE AGE

Making clothes from animal skins	Gathering roots, berries, and other edible plant food
Making shelters	Cooking
Making clay pots and vessels	Caring for children

NORTH AMERICAN WOMEN'S WORK IN 1492

Basket weaving	Cultivating berries and herbs for use as medicines to prevent or cure many illnesses
Food gathering	
Home building	
Sowing and harvesting corn and potatoes	Fashioning fur and leather into clothing
Catching and cooking fish and shellfish	Medicine women

A 1993 survey by Career and College *magazine found that most high school students wanted to be physical therapists, FBI agents, and accountants.*

If you're wondering, here's more to think about.

JOBS OF THE FUTURE

Lunar miner—It's thought that someday mines will be set up on the moon and people will be needed to mine these minerals and ship them back to earth.

Thanatologist—With an aging population, the need for more people to counsel and comfort the terminally ill will be necessary.

Orthotist—These people specialize in creating mechanical limbs and fitting them to patients with deformities or amputations.

Electric car mechanic—Environmentalists predict that the electric car will be the car of the future. These new cars will need to have their batteries recharged as well as regular maintenance, so there will be a need for electric car mechanics.

CRACKERJACK KIDS

Through history, some women have found their fame and fortune at a young age:

Writers

When Dorothy Straight of Washington, D.C. was 4 years old, she wrote a story for her grandmother entitled "How the World Began." Her parents thought it was good enough to be published. They were right. Dorothy's book was published in 1964, making her the youngest published author.

Hilda Conkling was 4 years old when she started writing poetry. She wrote poems daily and read them to her mother every evening. Her mother, a teacher at Smith College in Massachusetts, began sending the poems to magazines when Hilda was 8. In 1920, when she was 10, Hilda had one hundred poems collected and published in *Poems by a Little Girl*.

Phillis Wheatley was sold as a slave to a Boston family when she was 6 years old. She was taught to read, and by the time she was 13 she had written her first poem. When she was 15 she was reading Latin. She was the first black woman to publish poetry in the U.S. Her book, *Poems on Various Subjects, Religious and Moral,* was published in 1773.

Edna St. Vincent Millay began composing verse almost as soon as she could write. At first she copied down the poems she read in books. Soon she decided it would be more interesting to write her own. She went on to win the Pulitzer Prize for Poetry in 1923.

Anne Frank started writing in her diary on her thirteenth birthday while she and her family were in hiding from the Nazis. Anne kept up her diary while living in secrecy. A year later the family hiding place was betrayed and they were all sent to concentration camps. Anne died of typhus while imprisoned. The only one to survive was her father. He returned to their hideout, where he found Anne's diary. He had it published in 1947. To date, more than 13 million copies have been printed in more than 50 languages.

Like Anne Frank, 13-year-old Zlata Filipovic of Sarajevo kept a wartime diary. When she was 11, Zlata started her diary. Her first entries told of school work and birthday parties. When Serbian troops invaded her country, the entries changed to stories of bombings and death. Zlata's diary was bought by a French publishing company who helped her family escape from Sarajevo. In the spring of 1994, *Zlata's Diary* was published in the U.S.

American poet Gwendolyn Brooks's first collection of verse, *American Childhood* was written when she was 13 years old. In 1950 she became the first African American to win a Pulitzer Prize. She won for *Annie Allen,* which includes a poem describing the experiences of a black girl growing up in America.

Janis Ian was 13 when she wrote "Society's Child," a song about interracial love. The words and melody came to her while she was in school waiting to see her guidance counselor. Her recording of that

"We real cool. We
Left school. We
Lurk late. We
Strike straight. We
Sing sin. We
Thin gin. We
Jazz June. We
Die soon.

GWENDOLYN BROOKS, "WE REAL COOL" FROM *THE BEAN EATERS*

song sold in the millions. She was on the road performing when she was 16. By the time she was 24, she had a Grammy for another of her songs, "At Seventeen," which tells of teenage loneliness.

Emma Lazarus was a sickly child who spent most of her childhood at home alone. She was an avid reader and at 14 years old she began to write poetry. Her first book was published when she was 17. She is best known for her poem "The New Colossus" which is inscribed on the Statue of Liberty.

Louisa May Alcott was so determined to help her family financially that she taught school, sewed, and hired out as a houseworker when she was a teenager. Her passion was writing and at 18 she sold her first poem, "Sunlight." In the same year (1851) she began to sell her short stories for five dollars apiece. She continued to support her family with her writing. She is most famous for her novel *Little Women*.

A Magazine of Our Own

New Moon: The Magazine for Girls and Their Dreams is a bimonthly magazine put out by twenty-five girls between the ages of 8 and 14. The girls live in Duluth, Minnesota, where they write articles, draw pictures, and edit stories submitted by other girls from around the world. For a subscription, write to: New Moon, P.O. Box 3587, Duluth, Minnesota 55803.

Painters

Fede Galizia was born in Italy in 1578. By the time she was a teenager she was an accomplished portrait painter. She was famous throughout Europe.

Artemisia Gentileschi lived in Europe from 1593 to 1652. She was only 17 when she finished her well-known painting, *Susanna and the Elders*.

Angelica Kauffman was born in Switzerland in

1740. She began to paint with her father when she was just 11 years old. She soon achieved her own fame as a decorative painter of buildings. Some of her work can be seen today on buildings in London, England.

Performers

Shirley Temple was born in 1928. She began dancing as soon as she could walk. When she was 4 years old, her mother moved her from dancing classes into films. Her first movie was *The Red-Haired Alibi* (1932). When she was 6 years old she was awarded a special Oscar for her performance in the movie *Bright Eyes*. She danced, sang, and acted her way into the hearts of moviegoers. From 1935 to 1938 she was the most popular box office attraction in the U.S. As she grew up, her career faded; she stopped making movies in 1949. She married Charles Black in 1950 and in the 1960s began a political career. As Shirley Temple Black she became an American diplomat and the first woman appointed Chief of Protocol in the U.S. State Department.

Judy Garland was 7 years old when she began singing in vaudeville shows with her two sisters. At 13 she obtained a movie contract. At 14 she starred in *The Wizard of Oz*. She continued to sing in musical comedy movies throughout the '40s. When she died in 1969 at the age of 47, she had become a musical legend. More than 20,000 people attended her funeral.

Elizabeth Taylor was born in England in 1932. When she was 10 years old she began her acting career with a small part in *There's One Born Every Minute*. At 12 she starred in *National Velvet,* and at 17 she played the role of Amy in the movie version of *Little Women.* She continued to act and has won two Academy Awards as an adult.

Patty Duke opened on Broadway in *The Miracle Worker* when she was 13 years old. She played the role of Helen Keller. Two years later she starred in the film version of the play and won and Oscar for best supporting actress.

Tatum O'Neal was 10 years old when she won an Oscar for best supporting actress for her performance in *Paper Moon.* At that time, she was the youngest person ever to win.

Jodie Foster began her prolific acting career as a child, appearing in many Disney films and television programs. By the time she was 13 years old she had landed sophisticated roles in movies like *Taxi Driver* and *Bugsy Malone.* She continued her acting career while she earned a college degree and won best actress awards in 1988 for *The Accused* and in 1991 for *The Silence of the Lambs.*

Anna Paquin had never acted before her Oscar-winning performance in *The Piano.* She was 11 years old when she won the 1993 Oscar for best supporting actress.

Ethel Waters was born in 1900. She began singing in public when she was 5 years old. She was billed as a baby star when she began performing on the vaudeville circuit at the age of 8. She continued to sing and act as an adult, appearing in the Broad-

Two other successful girl actors are: Tina Majorini, a 9-year-old who appeared in When a Man Loves a Woman *and* Andre. *Zelda Harris, another 9-year-old, acted in Spike Lee's* Crooklyn.

way play *The Member of the Wedding* and in the film *Cabin in the Sky*. Her autobiography is *His Eye is on the Sparrow*.

American opera singer Beverly Sills was born in 1929. She was 3 years old when she began singing on a weekly radio show called "Bob's Rainbow Hour." When she was 17 her voice had such a range she was able to sing twenty opera arias.

British pop singer Petula Clark had her own radio show called "Pet's Parlour" when she was 11 years old. The show aired on BBC radio in 1943.

Gladys Knight was born in Atlanta in 1944. She debuted at the age of 4 singing solos in a Baptist Church. When she was 8, she was on the nationally televised *The Original Amateur Hour* singing popular songs. By 1957 she had joined with her brother and cousins to form the pop group The Pips, which later became Gladys Knight and the Pips.

Alison Krauss began playing the violin when she was 5 years old. She won the Illinois Fiddling Championship when she was 11. At 15 she had recorded her first solo album. By the time she was 17, this singer and bluegrass fiddler had made five albums, won two Grammys, and sold more than half a million records.

Dame Alicia Markova was born Alicia Marks in England in 1910. When she was 10 years old she made her first professional appearance as a ballet dancer in *Dick Whittington* at the Kennington Theater in London. By the time she was 14 she was dancing with the world famous Ballet Russe, the dance company of Serge Diaghilev. She danced the title role in Balanchine's *Lerossignol* when she was 16. Markova retired from dancing in 1963 and began to teach and to produce ballets.

American dancer Gelsey Kirkland was born in 1953. She was spotted by George Balanchine and asked to dance for his New York City Ballet when she was 15 years old. Within four years she became a principal dancer in the company. She later went on to dance for the American Ballet Company where she partnered such greats as Nureyev and Baryshnikov.

Movers and Shakers

Susan Boudinot is remembered as one of the youngest protesters in colonial America. When she was 9, she and her family were visiting the royal governor of New Jersey. She was offered a cup of tea, accepted it, curtsied, and tossed it out the window. She was boycotting British tea, which had been hurting the economy of colonial American merchants.

Sybil Luddington was 16 years old when she joined American Revolutionary War forces, riding 40 miles on horseback in the dark of night to obtain military reinforcements.

It was because of 11-year-old Grace Bedell that Abraham Lincoln became the first U.S. president to wear a beard. When Lincoln was running for president, she sent him a letter saying, "You would look a great deal better, for your face is so thin... [people] like whiskers and they would...vote for you and then you would be president." Lincoln was elected and, as photos show, he wore a beard. When the train taking Lincoln to Washington stopped in Grace's hometown of Westfield, New York, he met Grace and said, "You see, I let the whiskers grow for you, Grace."

The often quoted line, "Yes Virginia, there is a Santa Claus" comes from the response to a letter written by 8-year-old Virginia O'Hanlon. In 1897 she wrote a letter to the editors of the *New York Sun* newspaper asking if Santa Claus existed. The answer, written by the editor, appeared in the September 21, 1897, edition of the paper. It read: "Yes, Virginia, there is a Santa Claus. He exists as surely as love....How dreary would be the world if there was no Santa Claus! It would be as dreary as if there were no Virginias."

Samantha Smith was 10 years old when she was invited to the Soviet Union to meet with the Soviet leader Yuri Andropov in 1985. She had sent him a letter asking why his country seemed so belligerent to the rest of the world. Sadly, Samantha was killed in a plane crash on her return to Maine.

Prodigies

Maria Gaetana Agnesi was the first-born of twenty-one children. She lived in Milan, Italy, in the early 1800s. At the age of 5 she spoke fluent French. By 9 she spoke Latin, Greek, and Hebrew. She once delivered an hour-long speech to an academic gathering. The subject was the right of women to be educated, and the speech was written and spoken in Latin. Maria was 9 years old at

A prodigy is a person of exceptional power and ability. A child prodigy is a kid who is recognized for genius at an early age.

the time. By the age of 20 she had begun a major work on differential and integral calculus. She used her linguistic ability to bring together authors writing in various languages; she also formulated new methods for mathematics.

Hazel Scott was born in Trinidad in 1920. She began playing the piano at the age of 3. Her family moved to New York City when she was 4. At the age of 5 she debuted in a piano concert. When she was 8, she was accepted to the Juilliard School of Music on a 6-year scholarship. At that time, students had to be 16 to enter the school. By the time she was 13, Hazel was called the child wonder pianist. Hazel Scott died in 1981 after a lifetime of performing classical music, singing, and acting.

Sarah Caldwell, the highly esteemed opera conductor and producer, was born in 1928. She was recognized as a mathematical and musical prodigy at the age of 4. At 10 she was giving violin recitals. She played on her own radio show when she was 16. That same year she played with Count Basie's band at the Roseland Dance Hall in New York City. In 1957, with only five thousand dollars, she founded the Opera Company of Boston.

Olya Zaranika of Russia was 7 years old when she finished composing her second complete opera. In 1993, when Olya was 9, her first opera was staged in Moscow.

Dating and Mating

MOST PEOPLE IN THE WORLD get married. Some date to find their partner. Some have to  marry a partner already chosen for them. Dating and marriage ceremonies are surrounded by rituals and superstitions and are as varied as the cultures and people of the world.

INTERNATIONAL DATE-LINES

These are some of the ways teens date in other countries of the world.

Afghanistan

Dating is rare in Afghanistan because most marriages are arranged by parents, and schools are separate for boys and girls. The opportunities to meet are rare. Girls have a 7:00 P.M. curfew, while boys have an 11:00 P.M. curfew.

Australia

Most teens go out in large groups and don't pair off until they are 18 or 19 years old in Australia. Girls often ask out boys and pay for the date, too. Couples often go to dinner parties, barbecues, or the beach.

Central and South America

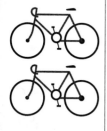

Dating is not allowed until the age of 15 here. When of age, most boys and girls date in large groups, going out together to weekend dance parties. When not dancing, teens gather at local clubs to eat and talk.

Europe

Dating is usually a group event in Europe. In Finland, as many as thirty teens may attend a movie together. Slumber parties are common in Italy and Switzerland, where teens gather for parties at a home and sleep there when the party is over.

In Spain teens join a *pandilla,* a club or a group of friends with the same interests, like cycling or hiking. Dating is done one-to-one and both girls and boys ask each other out and split the cost of the evening's entertainment.

In Russia dates take place at dances or at clubs where teens eat or chat with friends. In small towns, teens meet in the streets downtown or gather around a fountain.

Iran

It is against the law to date in Iran. Teens are separated until they are of marrying age, then their families introduce them to each other and sometimes a courtship follows.

Japan and Korea

In Japan and Korea, most high school students don't date or go to parties, but spend their time studying instead. Dating begins in college, when only boys do the asking and pay for the dates.

MARRIAGE THROUGH TIME

It is believed that the first "marriage" took place when a primitive man went into a primitive woman's cave and carried her off to be his mate. He chose her not for love but for her ability to do work. Since then, of course, the idea of marriage has changed quite a lot.

Ancient Greeks and Spartans

All marriages were arranged by parents and approved by the gods in ancient Greece. Women in their early teens were married to men in their mid-thirties. A husband then had to buy his new wife from her father. Many couples did not see each other until after the ceremony, when the bridal veil was removed. On the night before the wedding, the girl's hair was cut off and she was bathed in holy water from a sacred fountain. Her childhood toys were then taken away and dedicated to a goddess. Greek wives were "owned" by their husbands, who could lend or sell them to others.

The Spartans believed that a person's athletic ability matched their fitness for marriage. Before marrying, a couple was required to wrestle in public to show their compatibility. Spartan women mar-

ried in their twenties. The groom's father chose a bride for his son. Twelve months after the selection, the couple was married. During the marriage ceremony, the bride wore a white robe, a veil, and jewelry given to her by her new husband's family. The ceremony took place in the groom's tent and the festivities lasted seven days. If a woman was wealthy, she might have a husband for each house she maintained.

Romans
Roman brides wore white tunics with orange veils and orange slippers. Following the ceremony, the groom carried his bride over the threshold of their new home to symbolize his ownership of her.

Medieval Christians
Christian church marriages were thought to be made in heaven and therefore could never be broken. The father of the bride gave a dowry of land or money to the groom. If the marriage was unsuccessful, the wife and the dowry were returned to the father's home, but neither partner was allowed to remarry.

Ancient Japanese
Until the 1400s, married couples did not live together in Japan. They stayed in separate homes, meeting only at night. The old Japanese word for marriage meant, "slip into the house by night."

MARRIAGE TODAY

Amish
When an Amish couple wants to marry, the man asks a churchman to ask the woman's parents for

their approval. If consent is given, the marriage is announced two weeks before the wedding. The wedding takes place on a Tuesday or Wednesday in November, after the harvest. The bride wears white for the first and only time in her life. There are no rings, photographs, or flowers at the wedding. There is no honeymoon and the couple does not live together until the springtime, after a series of weekend visits with family and friends.

Arabs

Arab marriages are arranged between two families. They agree on the amount of money to be paid the bride's family for her trousseau (a wardrobe the bride acquires before marriage). An Arab bride celebrates her wedding in an ancient ceremony that excludes men. The bride's hair is covered with henna, a deep red dye, and her body is elaborately painted by her friends. Afterward the women all dance together.

French

In France, one couple may have three marriage ceremonies. The first is the civil ceremony, which is performed in the town hall with the mayor officiating. The second ceremony is religious, usually Roman Catholic, performed by a priest. The third takes place if the couple lives in the countryside. In this ceremony, the people of the village host a ten-course banquet for the bride and groom in which there is singing, storytelling, games, and toasting. The villagers bang pots and pans to remind the couple of the possible difficulties of marriage.

Germans

In a wedding ceremony in Germany, the bride and groom hold candles decorated with ribbons and flowers.

Greeks

At a Greek wedding ceremony a guest of honor known as the *koumbaros* crowns the wedding couple and joins them in a symbolic gesture by circling the alter three times.

Indians

Child marriages are still common in parts of rural India, where it is not unusual for 7-year-olds to marry! On the day of the ceremony, the young groom rides into town on a horse followed by hundreds of friends and relatives. A local wise man chants wedding *mantras,* or prayers. The bride and groom walk around a ceremonial fire seven times. The bride goes to live in her husband's house for three days. She then returns to her own house to await puberty, when she will be reunited with her husband.

Italians

After the wedding ceremony the newlyweds are showered with confetti made of sugar-coated almonds. This confetti symbolizes the bitterness and sweetness of married life.

Japanese

Japanese couples are traditionally introduced by a *nakodo,* or go-between, who is usually a friend or relative. The engagement is celebrated with a toast of sake and an exchange of presents such as seaweed, fish, fans, and thread. The most common wedding ceremony in Japan is the Shinto ceremony. The bride and groom sit at the altar of a shrine with their parents and the go-between. After being purified by a Shinto priest, the bride and groom each drink from three cups of sake three times. The bride wears a white kimono to symbolize the death of her ties to her own family. She also wears a special hat known as a horn cover to cover her horns of jealousy. The marriage is legal when the couple registers at a local government office.

Mbutis

These nomadic people live in Central Africa. A Mbuti man must prove his worth to a woman's parents by catching an antelope single-handedly and offering it to them. He also gives small gifts of roots, nuts, or birds, or orchids from the tops of the tallest trees in the forest. When the couple is ready to be married they build a house and live together. They are finally married three days after the bride gives birth to her first child.

WEDDING RITUALS

Most wedding traditions, like throwing rice and eating cake, started long ago. Here are some of the stories behind the rituals.

Bridal dress

- Wearing a new white dress to be used only for a wedding ceremony is a tradition that is only about 150 years old. Before that, few women could afford a dress they would wear only once.
- White traditionally symbolizes youth and innocence.

- Red and orange are popular in Asia and the Middle East, where they are considered joyful and festive colors.

Cake

- Using wheats and grains in the making of wedding cakes is an ancient symbol of fertility.
- In ancient Rome a thin loaf of bread was broken over the marrying couple's heads. The crumbs were saved and taken home by the guests as tokens of good luck.
- Tiered wedding cakes originated in old England, where the bride and groom kissed over a stack of little cakes.

Canopy

- The canopy used in Jewish weddings is called a *huppah*. The couple and the rabbi stand under the cloth canopy during the wedding ceremony; it is a symbol of the couple's future home.

Flowers

- Ancient Roman brides wore bunches of herbs under their veils as symbols of fidelity.
- Orange blossoms are symbols of happiness and fertility because the orange tree blooms and bears fruit at the same time.
- Roses are the flowers of love, making June, the month of roses, the most popular wedding month.
- The early Greeks believed ivy to be the sign of everlasting love. It is still used to trim wedding bouquets.

Flower girls

- Flower girls first appeared in wedding ceremonies in the Middle Ages. Two young girls—usu ally sisters—dressed alike, carried wheat before the bride in the procession. Later on, flowers replaced the wheat and it became customary for the flower girls to strew petals at the bride's feet.

Glass breaking

- At the end of a Jewish wedding ceremony a wine glass is covered with a white cloth and laid on the ground. The groom breaks it by stomping on it. This symbolizes the destruction of the ancient Jewish temple. It is a reminder of the seriousness of marriage and that it cannot be reversed.

Honeymoon

- This first vacation taken by a newly married couple dates back to very early times when a groom wanted to hide the wife he had captured.
- The Teutons, an ancient German tribe, gave the honeymoon its name. After the wedding ceremony, honey was drunk until the moon waned.

Rice throwing

- Rice is a symbol of fertility and long life. Guests throw it at the bride and groom as a wish for children and a good life. Other good luck charms are confetti, orange blossoms, corn, barley, chickpeas, and dates and figs to sweeten the marriage.

Rings

- Engagement rings originated from the custom of exchanging rings to seal an important agreement.
- Rings are circular and without end to symbolize eternal love.
- A wedding ring is worn on the third finger of the left hand because it was believed that a vein or

nerve ran directly from this finger to the heart.

Veils

- Roman brides wore veils 2,000 years ago. Veils were worn as a sign of modesty and secrecy and were removed only by the husband after the wedding ceremony.
- The first American woman to wear a wedding veil was Nelly Custis, Martha Washington's daughter. She wore the veil to please her husband-to-be, who had complimented her on how pretty she looked when seen through a lace-curtained window.
- In some Eastern countries a veil is placed between the man and woman throughout the wedding ceremony. This ensures that they cannot see or touch one another until after the marriage.

SUPERSTITIONS: LOVE LORE

A superstition is the belief that an object or an action will have influence on one's life. Folklore abounds with superstitions related to love and marriage; here are some of them.

Marriage superstitions

A bride can ensure good luck in her marriage by wearing something old, something new, something borrowed, and something blue.

It is bad luck for a bride and groom to see each other before the ceremony on their wedding day.

Marry in September's shine,
Your living will be rich and fine;
If in October you do marry,
Love will come but riches tarry;

Gypsies found the mule with the longest ears and asked it if they would fall in love soon. If the mule shook its head, the answer was yes; if the mule moved one ear, the answer was maybe; and if the mule did not move, the answer was no.

If you wed in bleak November,
Only joy will come, remember;
When December's showers fall fast,
Marry and true love will last.
Marry for wealth, Tuesday for health,
Wednesday the best day of all;
Thursday for crosses,
Friday for losses,
Saturday no luck at all.

Love superstitions

Sure-fire signs you'll fall in love soon:
• You stumble going up a flight of stairs.
• You have hairy legs.
• You dream of taking a bath.
• The lines on your palm form an *M*.

To dream of what your next boyfriend will look
like,

• Sleep with a mirror under your pillow.
• Wear your nightgown inside out.
• Rub your headboard with lemon peel before turn-
ing off the light.
• Count nine stars each night for nine nights.
• Put daisies under your pillow at night.
• Take a sprig of rosemary and a sprig of thyme.
Sprinkle them three times with water and place
each herb in a shoe. Put the shoes at the foot of
your bed.
• Stand in front of a mirror and brush your hair
three times.

Fashion and Dress

"SEEK THE FASHION WHICH truly fits and befits you. You will always be in fashion if you are true to yourself, and only if you are true to yourself."

—Maya Angelou

WHAT GOES AROUND COMES AROUND

Everything old is new again. In the world of fashion, most "new" looks have been around before. Here are some examples.

Unisex clothing

Women and men have worn the same clothing for centuries. Ancient Romans and Greeks wore tunics, so the unisex clothing of the '60s wasn't really new. The traditional clothing of China, India, Japan, and Malaysia has always been unisex. Some time during the Middle Ages women took off trousers and put on dresses, and gender-related fashions began.

Long tops over leggings

This popular women's wear of the '80s was worn in the fifteenth century by men as a tunic over tights, like Robin Hood and his band of merry men.

Platform shoes

The ancient Romans wore platform shoes to keep their feet out of the mud and water. Platform shoes were revived in the '30s, the '70s, and again in the '90s in the U.S.

Shaved Heads

Both Egyptian women and men shaved their heads. Unlike today, the ancients covered their shaved heads with wigs.

Bikinis

These two-piece bathing suits may have shocked the modern world when they appeared in Paris in 1946, but bikinis first appeared in a fourth-century mosaic in Sicily.

Topless
Egyptian noblewomen went topless. They wore tunics that wrapped below their breasts and were held up by a center strap. In 1964 topless swimsuits were fashionable. Women who wore them in the U.S., however, were arrested for indecent exposure.

Belly Bags
As far back as the Bronze Age, people attached bags to their belts to hold valuables.

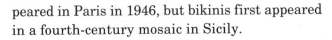

Body Piercing
From earliest times, piercing the ears, nose, and bellybutton has been a superstitious practice: the holes were thought to release demons from the body. In Europe during the Renaissance, wearing one earring was the fashion.

Stick-on adornments
Known as beauty patches, stick-ons date back to ancient Rome. Women wore small patches of adhesive cloth cut into the shapes of stars, crescent moons, and hearts on their cheeks, foreheads, and throats. During the Middle Ages, beauty patches were used to cover smallpox scars.

High-top sneakers
These canvas sneakers were first popular in 1930.

Pea coats
Navy pea coats first appeared in Army-Navy stores after World War II. Since then they have had pe-

riodic revivals, including a period in the 1960s when they were worn by hippies. Pea coats resurfaced yet again in the winter of 1994.

A FEW FASHION FIRSTS

1470   To hide her pregnancy, Queen Juana of Portugal wore the first hoop skirt.

1477   Anne of Burgundy became the first woman to receive a diamond engagement ring. It was given to her by Maximilian I of Germany.

1922   The first "flesh-colored" stockings are sold for women whose skin color is pinkish-beige. It was another twenty-five years before stockings for brown- and black-skinned women were available.

1938   Nylon stockings are invented. They are first sold in stores in 1940.

1940   Shoulder bags for women first appeared as part of service uniforms worn during World War II.

1960s   Fun furs of acrylic and polyester are made to look like real fur.

1960s   Paper clothes are made for the public. They are disposable and used for underwear and children's clothing.

1978   The first designer jeans are fashioned by Gloria Vanderbilt.

1980s   The wrinkled look is introduced. Wrinkles are permanently pressed into fabrics and shirts, vests, blouses, jackets, and pants.

1990s   Counterfeit clothing is made by computer, producing brand-name fakes. Polo, Guess?, Gap, Banana Republic, DKNY, and Disney are all copied.

DRESSED TO KILL

Virginia Woolf once said, "It's clothes that wear us, and not we them." As you will see, this can be downright dangerous.

- Throughout history, cosmetics made from mercury and lead disfigured faces and sometimes poisoned people to death.

- Hair dying, fashionable in ancient times, often resulted in total hair loss.

- When small feet were considered aristocratic and feminine, women squeezed their feet into the smallest possible shoes, causing the bones of their feet to become twisted and deformed.

- Tightly laced corsets made breathing and movement difficult.

- Hoop skirts made getting through a door difficult, getting into a carriage almost impossible, and, if the wearer sat down too fast, the hoop could fly up and break her nose.

- Layers of crinolines or hoops made falling down easy but getting up almost impossible.

- Wearing high heels has immobilized women and resulted in bunions, corns, twisted ankles, spinal deformities, and shortened calf muscles.

- The bustle of the 1900s, a rolled fabric attached to a woman's behind, made sitting down difficult.

- The hobble skirt of 1915 was so narrow below the knees that it made it difficult for women to walk.

SHADES OF FASHION

A colorful world is a world of meaning because people have always used color as symbols. Here are some of the ways fashion and color have connected.

Blonde

Blonde has long been a desirable hair color in many cultures. Natural blondes are rare among most of the world's population, so many people— even as long ago as the ancient Romans—have bleached their hair to make it blonde. In the 1990s blonde became the signature of many African American entertainers, who bleached their hair platinum blonde.

Blue

In Syria blue is the color for mourning.

In fifth-century Europe, blue colored scarves were worn around the neck to avoid infection during pregnancy.

Until the 1920s blue was considered a feminine color.

In the U.S., the color blue has long been associated with work clothes, thus the term "blue collar worker."

Green

Wearing green is thought to bring you tranquility and calm.

The landscape in Ireland is very green, it is the national color and the Irish believe it brings good luck.

Purple

Purple has always been considered the color of royalty, maybe because it was so hard to get. Cleopatra needed 20,000 snails soaked for ten days to obtain one ounce of purple dye for her royal clothing.

In Europe purple was the color of mourning used when the grieving period was half over.

Pink

Before the 1920s pink was considered a color for boys.

Shocking pink was named by designer Elsa Schiaparelli. She used bright pink in her clothing and named her perfume Shocking.

Red

The Aztecs of Mexico taught the Spanish how to obtain the color red by crushing insects called cochineals.

In the seventeenth century most shoes worn by the nobility had red heels.

Scarlet was originally the name of a fabric. Because it was so often dyed a brilliant red, the name became associated with the color rather than the material.

White

In China white is the color of mourning.

The tradition of brides in white for weddings only began in the nineteenth century. In the seventeenth and eighteenth centuries wearing white for a wedding was criticized. In ancient Rome, yellow was the usual wedding color. And in the Middle Ages there was no designated color for bridal wear.

WHO WEARS THE PANTS?

- In Asia both women and men have always worn pants for warmth, comfort, and convenience. In Rome and Greece women and men wore tunics.
- In the fourth century, women in the Western world wore pants, which they adapted from the Persians. At that time, pants were considered unmanly.
- By the Middle Ages in Europe women were wearing dresses and men were wearing breeches.
- After the French Revolution, men took off their high heels, silk stockings, and wigs and began wearing trousers.
- In the nineteenth century women put on trousers to ride horses, but they hid them by wearing full skirts on top.
- All trousers were pull-ons until the nineteenth century, when front closures using buttons were introduced.
- Jeans were the first trousers to put women and men on equal terms.
- Until 1970 it was not fashionable and sometimes against the law to wear pants in offices, classrooms, and restaurants in the U.S.

CLOTHES CALL

Bandannas

Bandanna is the Hindu word for tie-dye. In the 1700s bandannas were imported to England from India. They were square cloths with dark red or blue backgrounds sprinkled with white or yellow spots. The English used them as neckcloths and handkerchiefs.

Farthingale
A variation on the hoop skirt, a farthingale was a support that extended a skirt horizontally from the waist. The French equivalent of this structure was called a *pannier.*

Jersey
Jerseys are knitted shirts that originated on the island of Jersey in the English Channel. They are commonly worn for sports.

Jumpsuits
Also called boilers and sirens, these one-piece outfits were first worn in Britain during World War II nighttime air raids by civilians who worked to keep the lights out in London.

Negligee
This was once a term for any informal dress worn by women and men at home. Now the word describes women's sleep wear.

Nightclothes
These were first fashioned in the 1500s. Up until that time people either slept naked or in day clothes.

Petticoat
Meaning a small coat, petticoat was commonly used to describe a shirt. In the nineteenth century it came to mean a women's slip.

Plaid
Plaid is a Gaelic word for blanket. Woolen blankets made in checkered patterns were worn in the British Isles as outer garments to protect against cold weather.

Masks

Beginning in the sixteenth century, European women wore masks to protect themselves from the weather or to conceal their identities.

Sweaters

Both sweaters and sweatshirts are names for jerseys worn for sports. College jocks called them sweaters because they became soaked in sweat after strenuous physical activity.

Wardrobes

This word was first used to describe a room in which clothes were kept. Later it also meant a piece of furniture in which clothes are hung, and clothing itself.

THE INS AND OUTS OF UNDERWEAR

Undershirts come out

Undershirts and tank tops are true symbols of female fashion freedom. They were introduced in the mid 1800s to be worn by women when they began playing sports. The invention of the bicycle in the late 1880s insured the survival of the undershirt because it was worn for long outings.

The very first undershirts were made of wool to protect a woman's "delicate constitution."

The first undershirts to appear in the Sears, Roebuck and Company catalogs were made of cotton, had crocheted armholes, and were adorned with ribbons.

By the 1900s undershirts were made of silk and lace.

In the 1930s women chose the bra over the undershirt. Undershirts were considered kids' clothes.

In the 1940s and 1950s undershirts were worn primarily by men.

T-shirts were once worn under other clothing. Now they are worn all by themselves. They got their name because the short sleeves and long bottom give them the shape of the letter T.

Undershirts were the radical garment of the hippies in the '60s. Singer Janis Joplin wore undershirts and beaded necklaces on stage. In 1968 Gloria Steinem made the undershirt the feminist uniform. Many women began replacing their bras with the more comfortable T-shirts and threw their bras in the garbage to symbolize this fashion change. This was called bra burning.

In the 1980s fashion designers revived the undershirt as seductive feminine wear.

In 1992 undershirts were worn as formal wear.

Underpants

European women did not wear underpants until the early 1900s.

Briefs were once considered men's underwear only, until the 1970s when women began wearing them, too.

Men's boxer shorts became outerwear for women in the 1980s.

Panty raids were a fad on American college campuses in the '60s. Men would storm women's dormitories and take their underpants.

Other names for underpants: unmentionables, unwhisperables, scanties, undies, panties, bloomers, knickers, drawers, step-ins, indescribables, small clothes, underpinnings, and inside clothes.

FIGURE CONTROL

Corsets

Corsets and girdles were first worn outside of clothing. This is evident in many European national costumes, such as that of Bavaria.

The ancient Greeks were the first to wear girdles. They called them zones. A band of linen or soft leather was bound around a woman's waist and lower torso to shape and control her mid-body.

The iron corset was devised in 1579 and was worn by women for about 10 years. The first modern corset was made in Britain in the 1700s. A short and light corset was made in America in 1911 for women to have the freedom of movement to dance the tango.

In Florence during the Renaissance, Catherine de Medici decreed it bad manners to have a thick waist and designed a hinged corset that narrowed the waist to 13 inches.

Bras

The first bra or breast band was worn by the ancient Greeks. It was called a mastoeides ("shaped like a breast").

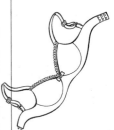

Bust improvers or padded bras were popular in 1840. These bras have been called falsies, cuties, bosom friends, waxen bosoms, lemon loves, and pneumatic breasts.

It wasn't until 1935 that bras were made with both cup and band sizes. The British called the cup measures junior, medium, full, and full with wide waist.

Strapless bras were introduced in 1938. They were popularized in the 1950s.

The sweater girl bra was made in the 1950s. Its cups were shaped to points and looked a lot like cones.

IF THE SHOE FITS—OR IF IT DOESN'T— WEAR IT!

The fashion for women has long been to have small delicate feet encased in high heels. This has made walking difficult, sometimes impossible. The sneakers and work boots worn by both sexes in the '80s and '90s liberated the feminine foot from fashionable bindings.

Footwear facts

- Sandals originated in warm climates where the soles of the feet needed protection but the top of the foot needed to be cool.
- 4,000 years ago the first shoes were made of a single piece of rawhide that enveloped the foot

for both warmth and protection.

- In Europe pointed toes on shoes were fashionable from the eleventh to the fifteenth centuries.
- In the Middle East heels were added to shoes to lift the foot from the burning sand.
- In Europe in the sixteenth and seventeenth centuries heels on shoes were always colored red.
- Shoes all over the world were identical until the nineteenth century, when left- and right-footed shoes were first made in Philadelphia.
- In Europe it wasn't until the eighteenth century that women's shoes were different from men's.
- Six-inch-high heels were worn by the upper classes in seventeenth-century Europe. Two servants, one on either side, were needed to hold up the person wearing the high heels.
- Sneakers were first made in America in 1916. They were originally called keds.
- Boots were first worn in cold, mountainous regions and hot, sandy deserts where horse-riding communities lived. Heels on boots kept feet secure in the stirrups.
- The first lady's boot was designed for Queen Victoria in 1840.

The Bata Shoe Museum, located in Toronto, Canada, is the only shoe museum in North America. The collection was compiled by Sonja Bata, of the Bata shoe-making family. The museum features shoes and shoe-related artifacts spanning 4,500 years.

Bata Shoe Museum
131 Bloor Street
West Toronto, Ontario, M5S 1R1

Shoes as symbols

- In Biblical times a sandal was given as a sign of an oath.
- In the Middle Ages a father passed his authority over his daughter to her husband in a shoe

ceremony. At the wedding, the groom handed the bride a shoe, which she put on to show she was then his subject.

- Today in the U.S. shoes are tied to the bumper of the bridal couple's car. This is a reminder of the days when a father gave the groom one of his daughter's shoes as a symbol of a changing care-taker.
- In China one of the bride's red shoes is tossed from the roof to ensure happiness for the bridal couple.
- In Hungary the groom drinks a toast to his bride out of her wedding slipper.

Hat pins, which were once used to hold large straw hats in place, can also be used as weapons against muggers.

TOPPING IT OFF WITH HATS

- "A hat makes all the difference" was a U.S. advertising slogan used in 1930. For centuries, tradition linked hats with female status. Married women and mothers were required to cover their heads with hats as signs of respectability. Unmarried women went bare-headed. Headwear is also a sign of power, from the crowns worn by royalty to the feathered head-dresses of tribal chiefs. Today, hats have become a fun topping. After a twenty-year lapse, they are back with a young, modern attitude.

Fun hats of the '90s

- Velvet floppies
- Woolly grunge caps
- Funky felt fedoras
- Perky trilbies
- Cold-weather balaclavas
- Wholesome baseball caps worn backwards
- Dr. Seuss–style stocking caps

- What's the difference between a bonnet, a cap, and a hat? The bonnet has no brim at the back and is usually tied under the chin. The cap fits closely to the head and doesn't have a brim, but it may have a visor. Hats vary in shape—they

111

may or may not have a brim, but they are usually grander than caps.

- Hats were worn everywhere—indoors and out—by women in the eighteenth century. They even wore a hat called a baigneuse in the bathtub.
- The term "feather in your cap" came from the American Indian tradition of obtaining feathers for headdresses. Birds were captured, some feathers plucked, and the birds were released. Each feather represented an act of bravery.
- The fashion of decorating hats with feathers declined in the twentieth century because too many birds were being slaughtered for their feathers. This is similar to the slaughter of elephants in recent years for their ivory tusks.

Modern mad hatters

- Artist Salvador Dali designed a woman's hat in 1930 that was shaped like a shoe with the inverted heel pointing upward. He also designed what he called a "madcap," which was shaped like a mountain peak.
- Designer Steven Jones created felt hats topped with a platter of fried eggs, sunnyside up. He also made hats that were simply metal colanders inverted on the wearer's head.
- Designer Anna Sui created teddy bear hats — whole bear heads that sit on the crown of the head.

Name that hat

These hats were well named, as their shapes show:

- Conversation hat (one side of the brim turned back and the other pulled forward)
- Beehive bonnet
- Pillbox
- Cloche (French for bell)

- Porkpie
- Turban
- Stocking cap

ALL MADE UP

Women and men have always used paints, powders, dyes, and perfumes to decorate their hair, faces, and bodies. From earliest times, colorful makeup was used to frighten enemies, to show social rank, for religious ceremonies, in puberty rites, to make magic, and to protect the skin and eyes.

A peek at the history of cosmetics

Egypt and Rome, 1,000 B.C.

- Women and men both used rouge, lipstick, and nail polish.

- Black and green eyeshadow was used to protect the eyes from the desert sun.
- Women traced the veins in their skin with blue paint.
- Black kohl was used as mascara, eyebrow darkener, and eyeliner.
- Body moisturizers included sesame, olive, palm, and almond oils.
- Perfumes were made of musk, thyme, myrrh, and frankincense.
- Hair dyes were made from henna, the blood of black cows, and from crushed tadpoles in warm oil.
- The first frosted look in makeup was achieved by pulverizing ant eggs and adding them to face paints.

Lipstick was first manu-factured in the U.S. in 1915. Kiss-proof lip-stick came out in 1925. Purple was the color of the '60s and white lip-stick was popular in the '70s.

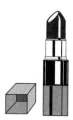

- The Romans used crocodile excrement for mud baths, barley flour and butter for pimples, and sheep fat and blood for nail polish.
- Roman men and women frequently dyed their hair blonde. The dyes were so caustic that many people lost their hair and had to wear wigs.
- In the Middle Ages, European society women painted their faces white or were bled (actually had some of the blood drained out of their bodies) to achieve a pale complexion.
- In China and Japan rice powder paint was used to paint faces white. Eyebrows were plucked, and teeth were painted black or gold.
- In Europe in the Middle Ages, beauty patches worn on the skin had meaning. Adhesive fabrics cut in the shapes of stars, hearts, and crosses were worn in the following manner: one to the right of the mouth meant the woman was flirtatious; one on the right cheek meant she was married; one on the left cheek meant she was engaged; and at the corner of an eye meant she was passionate.
- In Elizabethan England dyed red hair was the fashion. Women also slept with slices of raw beef on their faces to get rid of wrinkles.
- European men stopped using perfumes and wearing cosmetics during the Victorian era in England.

GLOVES

- In ancient times gloves were worn to protect working hands.
- In the Middle Ages gloves were worn as a sign of

wealth and power. Common people wore mittens.

- In the nineteenth century, society women and men wore gloves indoors and out. Black silk gloves were worn indoors during the daytime; white gloves were worn out at night.

Many social customs involved gloves.
- Gloves were surrendered as a forfeit for an error or a crime.
- Gloves were given as party favors at weddings.
- Knights in armor carried gloves as talismans in their helmets during tournaments. The gloves belonged to a loved one.
- Gloves were used as a pledge.
- Gloves were thrown down as a challenge.

CROSS-DRESSING FOR SASS AND SURVIVAL

"The thousand perplexities of fashionable Dress, wear so upon the temper of a woman, that she cannot be amiable." So wrote Mary Edwards Walker, a Civil War surgeon and journalist. She felt that nineteenth century women's dress was both ridiculous and inhumane, so she chose to dress in men's attire all the time. Other notable women who dressed in menswear can be found below. As you will see, most dressed as men to pursue their dreams in a male-dominated society.

Agnodice was the first known woman gynecologist. She lived in Greece in the fourth century B.C. In order to attend medical classes and to practice medicine she had to disguise herself as a man. She was accused and convicted of unlawfully practicing medicine because she was a woman.

Joan of Arc wore men's clothing to convince the French king to let her lead his army into battle. She was tried not only for treason but also for dressing as a man, which was a Roman Catholic offense. She was burned at the stake.

Mary Read, a British pirate, was first dressed as a boy by her mother in order to obtain financial help from her grandmother, who would only give money to a grandson. Later, Mary went to sea disguised as a man; she also served as a soldier and cavalry trooper. When she married, she wore women's clothes until her husband died, when once again she went to sea dressed as a man.

Deborah Sampson disguised herself as a man and enlisted as a soldier in the Revolutionary War under the name Timothy Thayer. When someone discovered she was a woman and she was thrown out of the army, she reenlisted under another name, Robert Shurtleff. When she was wounded in battle, a nurse discovered she was a woman.

George Sand, one of the most successful writers of the nineteenth century, was born Amandine Aurore Lucie Dupin. When she was a teenager, her free spirit led her to wear men's clothing. At 19 she was married and had two children. She left her family at age 27 and went to Paris, where she published her first novel under her pen name, George Sand.

FASHION FLASH

A decade-by-decade look at women's fashion in America.

1900s

- tight collars
- duster coats (long, lightweight driving coats worn to keep the dust off when riding in early automobiles on dirt roads)

1910s

- trenchcoats
- sneakers (first sports shoes, worn only for sports or during the day. They were never ever worn at night)
- V-neck sweaters

1920s

- cloches (bell-shaped, close-fitting hats with tiny brims)
- T-strap shoes
- flapper-style cocktail dresses
- short skirts
- bobbed hair

1930s

- nylon stockings
- wool-knit one-piece bathing suits
- hostess gowns
- padded shoulders

1940s

- rolled-up blue jeans
- eisenhower jackets (patch-pocketed battle

"Ugly" was the name of an extra brim attached to the front of a woman's bonnet. Uglies protected the eyes from sunlight.

117

jackets first worn by General Eisenhower during World War II)
- sloppy joe sweaters (baggy pull-on sweaters)

1950s

- capri pants (first worn in Capri, Italy, these were tight, calf-length pants with slits on the outside bottoms of the legs)
- motorcycle jackets
- pedal pushers (calf-length slacks worn by women and girls, originally worn by bicyclists)
- wraparound dresses
- jewel-studded flat shoes
- poodle skirts (felt skirts with poodle appliques)
- full skirts with petticoats
- baby doll pajamas
- strapless evening gowns

1960s

- unisex dressing
- miniskirts
- catsuits (tight-fitting, one-piece black suits)
- T-shirts with messages
- black suede flat shoes
- front-tied ballerina shoes
- the go-go look (white plastic or vinyl boots and short dresses originated by the go-go dancers at discotheques)
- tights for warmth, not fashion
- pantyhose
- poorboy sweaters

1970s

- Tank tops (sleeveless T-shirts)
- T-shirts worn with sweaters
- track suits
- T-shirts with logos
- pantsuits
- hot pants (named by *Women's Wear Daily,* these were very tight short shorts that made women look "hot")

1980s

- power suits (man-tailored business suits worn by women who were entering the professional workplace in large numbers for the first time in history)
- spandex bicycle shorts
- belly bags or fanny packs

1990s

- Terry cloth jackets
- Metallic leather or bright colored suede thongs
- Sneakers for evening wear
- Oversized sweaters with leggings
- Light-up sneakers
- Apron dresses
- Coaches' jackets
- Zip code T-shirts from popular, prestigious places
- Platform sneakers

FASHIONS NAMED FOR WOMEN

Betsy
A betsy is a ruffle or collar with rows of lace. It is named after Queen Elizabeth I of England.

Bloomers
Bloomers were named for Amelia Bloomer, the feminist who encouraged women to wear them because of the freedom of movement they allowed. The bloomer costume consisted of a simple flaring skirt over Turkish-style trousers. Bloomer did not design these and wasn't the first to wear them, but she promoted them in the U.S. and England. After she featured them in her magazine, women began wearing them for bicycling.

Jersey Lily
This is a wool jersey blouse worn over a pleated skirt. The outfit is named for Lillie Langtry, an English actress in the 1880s known as the Jersey Lily.

Juliet Cap
This is a small, close-fitting cap, usually made of lace set with pearls. It is named for Shakespeare's heroine Juliet, of *Romeo and Juliet* fame. Today the cap is worn as part of bridal or other formal wear.

Miranda Pump
This is a platform shoe with a flaring heel named after the entertainer Carmen Miranda. She was a popular movie star of the 1930s and 1940s.

Mother Hubbard
This is a loose dress, usually fitted only through

the shoulders and customarily worn while doing
chores. It is named for the nursery rhyme character whose cupboard was bare.

Palatine
This is a small cape made of lace or fur worn
around the neck. It is named after Princess Charlotte of the Palatine who tried to get women to be
more modest in their dress and brought this garment to France from Germany in 1676.

Pocahontas Dress
This is a suede or buckskin dress trimmed with
beads and fringe. It is named for the Algonquin
Indian princess named Pocahontas.

Pompadour
In the eighteenth century, the Marquise de Pompadour gave her name to a hairstyle in which the
hair is swept up high off the forehead.

THE LOOK OF HER

Gibson girl
A popular look in the early 1900s created by
Charles Dana Gibson. The Gibson girl wore a
starched, tailored shirtwaist with an ascot tie at
the neck and a floor-length skirt. With her hour-
glass figure, she was America's first pin-up girl.

Flapper
The American flapper first appeared in the 1920s.
She had short hair and wore a sleeveless chemise
with pleated flounces from hip to knee. To complete the outfit she wore ropes of pearls around her
neck and a cloche hat.

Bonnie and Clyde

This style of dressing got its inspiration from the movie *Bonnie and Clyde*. Bonnie Parker's outfit included a pinstripe "gangster" suit jacket from the 1930s, an above the knee skirt, and a beret worn to the side.

Ivy Leaguer

This look first appeared in the 1950s and was worn by students at prestigious Eastern colleges. The button-down collar is the trademark of this style.

Granny

This is a counterculture look cultivated by teenage girls in the 1960s. They wore long, loose, old fashioned dresses dowdy enough for their grandmothers to wear.

Hippie

This 1960s look started out as a fashion rebellion. The costume consisted of tie-dyed shirts, old jeans, black tights, lovebeads, and peace symbols. Hippies were also known as flower children.

Annie Hall

Someone dressed in this style wore baggy pants or a challis skirt and tried to look uncoordinated. This way of dressing was inspired by the 1970s movie of the same name that starred Diane Keaton.

Preppie

This conservative style of dress was favored by well-educated, affluent, city-dwelling Americans in the 1980s. It included upscale knee socks and saddle shoes, and imitated the kind of clothes worn by preparatory school students or graduates.

FROM HEAD TO TOE

Some fashions were created by influential women who tried to hide their own physical flaws. The rise of long skirts in the fifteenth century, for instance, is attributed to King Louis XI of France's daughters' desire to cover their legs. And Queen Elizabeth I helped to popularize the high collar by wearing one to hide her spindly neck. Young girls living two hundred years ago were expected to cover themselves from head to toe. Twelve layers to be exact! And you thought it took *you* a long time to get dressed! Here are the layers:

1. a frilly undershirt

2. a bodice with lots of buttons

3. a garter belt to hold up stockings

4. long stockings

5. long underpants that were buttoned to the bodice

6. shoes

7. a red flannel petticoat

8. a starched petticoat

9. a dress

10. an apron

11. a hair ribbon

12. a bonnet

DESIGNING WOMEN

Couture designers are the trendsetters of fashion. Madame Paquin of France was the first woman in haute couture, meaning "high sewing" or the best sewing, it now means "high fashion." Madame Paquin opened her shop in Paris in 1891. She specialized in elegant evening gowns trimmed in gold and fur. She was the first to show her clothes using a dressmaker's dummy, or mannequin.

In the 1800s some women protested against the corset, dressing themselves and their daughters in large shapeless garments. Famous among these women were the poet Christina Rossetti and the writer E. Nesbit.

Mary Jacobs, an American socialite, was responsible for some of the most important changes in women's underwear. In 1913, Mary bought an expensive evening gown that required an undergarment. Not happy wearing a corset, she created a backless bra from two white handkerchiefs, a strand of pink ribbon, and a cord. Any friends who admired her innovation received one as a gift. In 1914 she was awarded a patent for the first backless brassiere. Shortly after that she was contacted by the Warner Brothers Corset Company, offering to buy her patent rights for $1,500. She accepted their offer. The patent has since been valued at more than 20 million dollars.

Jeanne Lanvin (1867–1946) was famous for creating the unfitted, chemise-style flapper dress. Her House of Lanvin set the standard for fashion in the 1920s.

Gabrielle "Coco" Chanel (1883–1970) is considered the most significant designer of the twentieth century. She was responsible for introducing the little black dress, sweater sets, the pleated skirt, triangular scarves, and fake pearl necklaces; she pioneered the use of knit jersey as a fashion fabric; and she produced the first artificial suntan lotion. In addition, she marketed her own perfume called Chanel No. 5. Coco Chanel was a genius in her field. She was able to take an ordinary garment and transform it into a new fashion statement. She changed black from a color of mourning to a color of elegance. It is said that Chanel knew what women wanted to wear before they knew it themselves.

Elsa Schiaparelli (1890–1973) became famous for designing innovative, elegant clothes. Her dresses and suits of the 1930s with squared, padded shoulders changed the female figure. She originated the idea of separates for sports clothes. She was the first designer to use zippers and man-made fabrics for her fashions. Ms. Schiaparelli was also known for her use of strong and bright colors.

Mary Quant (1934–) turned the fashion world upside-down with her outrageous styles. She is credited with creating both the mod look of the 1960s and the miniskirt. Ms. Quant was awarded the Order of the British Empire for her services to fashion in 1966. She received this honor wearing a miniskirt.

Diane Von Furstenberg (1946–) is the creator of the now classic V-neck jersey wraparound dress. During the 1970s she was selling 20,000 of these dresses a week.

Liz Claiborne (1929–) made her name in sportswear. Her strength is in turning trends into wearable and salable clothes.

Chanel No. 5 was named after Coco's lucky number, 5. She was born on August 5, 1883.

Donna Karan (1948–) was an immediate success with the invention of bodysuit dressing. The bodysuit is worn underneath a long or short skirt and blouse, creating a complete outfit. Her collection of clothes is sleek, modern, and is worn by a wide range of people. Her company, DKNY (Donna Karan New York), is known for its classic sportswear look consisting of blazers, wide-legged pants, and chic dresses.

Girl Talk

TALK IS FUN. WE TALK ON the phone, talk  in class, talk to

Hello!

ourselves, talk things up, talk about what he or she said. You'll find lots worth talking about right here.

TALK ABOUT GIRLS

"Let our girls feel that we expect something more of them than that they merely look pretty and appear well in society. Teach them that...the world needs and is already asking for their...forces."
ANNA JULIA COOPER (1868–1964), AMERICAN EDUCATOR

"To grown people a girl of fifteen and a half is a child still; to herself she is very old and very real; more real, perhaps, than ever before or after."
FROM *THE BOARDWALK,* BY MARGARET WIDDEMER (1880–1978)

"If a girl...wants enough to learn, she will learn. It is hard but she was born to hardness—she cannot dodge it."
MARIA MITCHELL (1818–1889), AMERICAN ASTRONOMER

"Girls enforce the cultural code that men invent."
CLAUDIA DREIFUS (1944–), AMERICAN LABOR ORGANIZER, WRITER

"It occurred to me when I was thirteen and wearing white gloves and Mary Janes and going to dancing school, that no one should have to dance backward all their lives."
JILL RUCKELSHAUS (1937–), AMERICAN GOVERNMENT OFFICIAL

"'Did little girls have to be as good as that?' Laura asked and Ma said: 'It was harder for little girls. Because they had to behave like little ladies all the time, not only on Sundays. Little girls could never slide downhill, like boys. Little girls had to sit in the house and stitch on samplers.'"
LITTLE HOUSE IN THE BIG WOODS (1932) BY LAURA INGALLS WILDER

WHO SAID THAT?

"If the people have no bread, let them eat cake."
MARIE ANTOINETTE, FRENCH QUEEN, 1770

"My candle burns at both ends."
EDNA ST. VINCENT MILLAY, AMERICAN POET

"Laugh, and the world laughs with you. Weep, and you weep alone."
ELLA WHEELER WILCOX, AMERICAN POET

"Too much of a good thing can be wonderful."
MAE WEST, AMERICAN ACTOR

MARIE ANTOINETTE

"I cannot and will not cut my conscience to fit this year's fashions."
LILLIAN HELLMAN, AMERICAN WRITER

"I never said, 'I want to be alone.' I only said, 'I want to be left alone.' There is all the difference."
GRETA GARBO, AMERICAN ACTOR

"I was the horse and the rider."
MAY SWENSON, AMERICAN POET

"Home wasn't built in a day."
JANE ACE, AMERICAN RADIO PERSONALITY

"A woman without a man is like a fish without a bicycle."
GLORIA STEINEM, AMERICAN WRITER, FEMINIST

"Why do we kill people who are killing people to show that killing people is wrong?"
HOLLY NEAR, AMERICAN POLITICAL ACTIVIST

Catch Phrases

Catch phrases are slogans or expressions that are now widely used.

The lost generation
—Gertrude Stein, American author

Rainbow tribe
—Josephine Baker, American performer

Can we talk?
—Joan Rivers, American comedian

The sisterhood is powerful.
—Kathie Sarachild, American activist

"Gossip is the opiate of the oppressed."
ERICA JONG, AUTHOR OF *FEAR OF FLYING*

"I just told my mother I want a bra. Please help me grow God. You know where."
FROM *ARE YOU THERE GOD? IT'S ME, MARGARET,* BY JUDY BLUME

WOMANIST WORDS

Womanist words are those words that express a belief in and a respect for women and their talents. In her book *In Search of Our Mothers' Gardens: Womanist Prose,* Alice Walker defines "womanist" as: "Loves music. Loves dance. Loves the moon. Loves the Spirit. Loves love and food and roundness. Loves struggle. Loves the Folk. Loves herself. Regardless." Check out these womanist words:

VIRGINIA WOOLF

"Men their rights and nothing more; women their rights and nothing less."
SUSAN B. ANTHONY, AMERICAN SUFFRAGIST

"Womanhood is the great fact in her life; wifehood and motherhood are but incidental relations."
ELIZABETH CADY STANTON, AMERICAN SUFFRAGIST

"As a woman I have no country... As a woman my country is the whole world."
VIRGINIA WOOLF, ENGLISH AUTHOR

"Male supremacy has kept woman down. It has not knocked her out."
CLARE BOOTHE LUCE, AMERICAN DIPLOMAT

"I have met brave women who are exploring the outer edge of human possibility, with no history to guide them, and with a courage to make them-

selves vulnerable that I find moving beyond words."
GLORIA STEINEM, AMERICAN WRITER

"Feminism is about choices. It is about women choosing for themselves which life roles they wish to pursue, not being pushed into little wife/mother or... smart-but-not-sexy boxes by our society. It is about deciding who does and gets and merits and earns and succeeds in what, by smarts, capabilities and heart—not by gender. It is about honoring individuals because of their humanity, not their physiology."
ANNA QUINDLEN, AMERICAN WRITER

"The hen also knows when day breaks, but she lets the rooster announce it."
ASHANTI PROVERB

ZINGERS
Zingers are verbal punches. In this case, they are things said about men by women.

"Women want mediocre men, and men are working hard to be as mediocre as possible."
MARGARET MEAD, AMERICAN ANTHROPOLOGIST

"The trouble with some women is that they get all excited about nothing... and then marry him."
CHER, AMERICAN SINGER AND ACTOR

"Whatever women must do they must do twice as well as men to be thought half as good. Luckily this is not difficult."
CHARLOTTE WHITTON, CANADIAN MAYOR

"If you want anything said, ask a man. If you want

anything done, ask a woman."

MARGARET THATCHER, FORMER PRIME MINISTER OF ENGLAND

"There is only one free person in this society, and he is white and male."

HAZEL SCOTT, AMERICAN PIANIST

"A woman's two cents worth is worth two cents in the music business."

LORETTA LYNN, AMERICAN SINGER

"In those days, it didn't matter [if you were] a Phi Beta Kappa, Miss America, a Nobel Peace Prize winner, [if you weren't married or about to be] you were considered no more than half a woman."

BILLIE JEAN KING, AMERICAN TENNIS PLAYER

SLINGING SLANG

Here are some fun words to use to "spike" your conversations.

Brainrinse	To immobilize and pressure someone verbally.
Dak	A term of endearment for a true love.
Eyes only	A code on a private document. For the reader only.
Exudiate	To sweat.
Fathometer	What you need when you are totally perplexed.
Go-nogo	To change your mind in a stop and start fashion.
Kakatopia	An ugly place to live.
Slurb	A poorly designed suburb.
Unperson	Someone who is completely ignored and on the outs.
Yatata	Idle chatter

TALKING TRASH, OR
TALKING THROUGH YOUR HAT

When Napoleon Bonaparte said "women should stick to knitting" he was surely talking trash. Surprisingly, here are some quotes from women that also fit the category.

"One can never be too thin or too rich."

WALLIS SIMPSON WINDSOR (1896–1986), AMERICAN-BORN ENGLISH DUCHESS

"I'm a wonderful housekeeper. Every time I get a divorce, I keep the house."

ZSA ZSA GABOR (1919–), HUNGARIAN AMERICAN ACTOR

"I love men, not because they are men, but because they are not women."

QUEEN CHRISTINA OF SWEDEN (1626–1689)

"Make me a saint by getting meals, and washing up the plates!"

FROM "THE DIVINE OFFICE OF THE KITCHEN" BY CECILY HALLACK, ENGLISH WRITER, POET

"So this gentleman said, 'A girl with brains ought to do something else with them besides think.'"

FROM *GENTLEMEN PREFER BLONDES* (PUBLISHED IN 1925), BY ANITA LOOS

"I thank God for high cheekbones every time I look in the mirror in the morning."

SUZY PARKER (1933–), AMERICAN MODEL

FLOWER POWER

If you send someone a single rose you are sending a message of love. You can send all kinds of messages with flowers. Florigraphy is the language of flowers. Hundreds of flowers and trees have been given meanings and here are some of them.

FLOWER/TREE	MEANING
AMERICAN ELM	Patriotism
AMERICAN LINDEN	Matrimony
ANEMONE	Expectation
APPLE	Temptation
ARBORVITAE	Unchanging friendship
ASH TREE	Grandeur
ASPEN TREE	Lamentation
AZALEA	Temperance
BEECH TREE	Prosperity
BIRCH TREE	Meekness
BLUEBELL	Constancy
BUTTERCUP	Ingratitude
CHAMOMILE	Energy in adversity
CANDYTUFT	Indifference
CARNATION (RED)	Alas! My poor heart!
CEDAR	Strength
CHERRY TREE	Good education
CHRYSANTHEMUM	Slighted love
CLEMATIS	Mental beauty
COREOPSIS	Always cheerful
CYCLAMEN	Shyness
CYPRESS	Mourning
DANDELION	Wisdom
DAFFODIL	Regard
DAISY	We feel the same
DOGWOOD	Durability
ELM	Dignity

FLOWER/TREE	MEANING
FIG TREE	Prolific
FORGET-ME-NOT	True love
FUCHSIA	Taste
GERANIUM	Comfort
HOLLYHOCK	Ambition
HONEYSUCKLE	Generosity
HORSE CHESTNUT	Luxury
HYDRANGEA	Heartlessness
IRIS	Power
IVY	Fidelity
JUNIPER	Protection
LILAC	First Love
LILY OF THE VALLEY	Return of joy
LOCUST	Elegance
LUPINE	Imagination
MAGNOLIA	Love of nature
MORNING GLORY	Affectation
MULBERRY	Wisdom
NASTURTIUM	Patience
OAK TREE	Hospitality
ORANGE TREE	Generosity
PEAR TREE	Comfort
PLUM TREE	Fidelity
POPLAR	Courage
ROSE	Love
SUNFLOWER	Haughtiness
SWEET PEA	Delicate pleasure
SYCAMORE	Curiosity
TULIP	Fame
VIOLET	Faithfulness
WALNUT TREE	Intellect
WEEPING WILLOW	Mourning
ZINNIA	Absent friends

The first flower dictionary, Le Langage des Fleurs, *was written by Mme. Charlotte de la Tour (the pen name of Louise Cortambert) and published in Paris in 1818.*

SHE SAID THIS ABOUT THAT

Adventure

"I could not, at any age, be content to take my place in a corner by the fireside and simply look on. Life was meant to be lived."

ELEANOR ROOSEVELT (1884–1962), FIRST LADY, HUMANITARIAN

Advice

"Advice is what we ask for when we already know the answer but wish we didn't."

ERICA JONG (1942–), AMERICAN AUTHOR OF *FEAR OF FLYING*

Childhood

"The only thing I ever really wanted when I was a

ELEANOR ROOSEVELT

child was to be normal. To be average. To be able to run, jump, play and do all the things the other kids did in my neighborhood."

WILMA RUDOLPH (1940–1994), WHO WAS CRIPPLED AT 11 YEARS OLD, BUT WENT ON TO BECOME AN OLYMPIC MEDALIST IN TRACK AND FIELD AT AGE 20.

Dreams

"Thus, learning to understand our dreams is a matter of learning to understand our heart's language."

ANN FARADAY (1935–), AMERICAN PSYCHOLOGIST AND DREAM RESEARCHER

Hollywood

"It always sounds glamorous when you're young."

PATRICIA NEAL (1926–), AMERICAN ACTOR

AUNG SAN SUU KYI

Human rights

"It is not enough merely to call for freedom, democracy and human rights. There has to be a united determination to persevere in the struggle, to make sacrifices in the name of enduring truths, to resist the corrupting influence of desire, ill will, ignorance and fear."

AUNG SAN SUU KYI (1945–), BURMESE WRITER, WINNER OF THE NOBEL PEACE PRIZE, 1991

Jumping

"Jumping has always been the thing to me. It's like leaping for joy."

JACKIE JOYNER-KERSEE (1962–), AMERICAN TRACK AND FIELD ATHLETE AND OLYMPIC MEDALIST

Life

"We write our own destiny. We become what we do."

MADAM CHIANG KAI-SHEK (1898–), CHINESE SOCIOLOGIST

Love

"Love is much nicer to be in than an automobile accident, a tight girdle, a higher tax bracket, a flight pattern over Philadelphia."

JUDITH VIORST (1931–), AMERICAN WRITER

Pain and sorrow

"I've been in Sorrow's kitchen and licked out all the pots."

ZORA NEALE HURSTON (1901–1960), AMERICAN WRITER

Painting

"I found I could say things with color and shapes that I couldn't say in any other way—things I had no words for."

GEORGIA O'KEEFFE (1887–1986), AMERICAN PAINTER

Photography

"I really believe there are things nobody would see if I didn't photograph them."

DIANE ARBUS, AMERICAN PHOTOGRAPHER (1923–1971)

Poverty

"I might have been born in a hovel but I am determined to travel with the wind and the stars."

JACQUELINE COCHRAN (1910–1981), AMERICAN PILOT

Self

"Don't compromise yourself. You're all you've got."

JANIS JOPLIN (1943–1970)

Writing

"I want to be able to write so powerfully that I can break the heart of the world and heal it."

DOROTHY ALLISON (1949–), AMERICAN NOVELIST

JUMP ROPE JIVE

About a hundred years ago most jump rope jumpers were boys. Each boy had his own rope and jumped in competition with other boys. When girls took to jumping rope, they made it a group game and added rhythm and song. Here are some jump rope songs:

Candy, candy in the dish,
How many pieces do you wish?
1, 2, 3...

Two in the middle and two at the end,
Each is a sister and each is a friend.
A penny to save and a penny to spend,
Two in the middle and two at the end.

Sugar, salt, pepper, cider,
How many legs has a bow-legged spider?
1, 2, 3, 4...

Apple on a stick.
Five cents a lick.
Every time I turn around
It makes me sick.

Ice cream soda, Delaware punch.
Spell the initials of your honeybunch.
A, B, C...

Rooms for rent,
Inquire within.
As I move out,
Let _____ come in.

All in together, girls.
How do you like the weather, girls?
January, February, March, April...
(Jumpers run in on their birthday months)

SHE SAID IT IN SONG

- "O beautiful for spacious skies, For amber waves of grain," from "America the Beautiful" (1893) by Katherine Lee Bates
- "Twinkle twinkle little star, how I wonder what you are," from "The Star" (1806) by Ann Taylor
- "Swing low sweet chariot, Coming for to carry me home," from "Swing Low, Sweet Chariot" (1847) by Sarah Hannah Sheppard
- "Mine eyes have seen the glory of the coming of the Lord," from "Battle Hymn of the Republic" (1862) by Julia Ward Howe
- "Shine on, shine on harvest moon up in the sky," from "Harvest Moon" (1908) by Nora Bayes

- "Happy Birthday to you, Happy Birthday to you," from "Happy Birthday" (1893) by Patty Smith Hill
- "Mama may have/Papa may have/But God bless the child that's got his own," from "God Bless the Child" (1941) by Billie Holiday
- "When my soul was in the lost-and-found/You came along to claim it." from "A Natural Woman" (1967) by Carole King
- "Nothing cures like time and love," from "Time and Love" (1970) by Laura Nyro
- "If I have to, I can do anything/I am strong, I am invincible," from "I Am Woman" (1972) by Helen Reddy

- "Sometimes this face looks so funny/that I hide it behind a book," from "Either or Both" (1973) by Phoebe Snow
- "You're so vain, I bet you think this song is about you," from "You're So Vain" (1972) by Carly Simon
- "We are stardust/We are golden," from "Wood-

stock" (1975) by Joni Mitchell

- "Now that I have won my freedom, like an eagle,/ I am eager for the sky," from "Light of a Clear Blue Morning" (1976) by Dolly Parton
- "Ask me if you want to know the way to Coolsville," from "Coolsville" (1979) by Rickie Lee Jones
- "My mama told me.../She say don't give or sell your soul away," from "All That You've Got Is Your Soul" (1989) by Tracy Chapman
- "Strong steppin', struttin', moving and not forgettin' we are the ones who gave birth to the new generation of prophets," from "Ladies First" (1991) by Queen Latifah
- "If a child lives with money he learns to spend his time," from "Mama Help Me" (1992) by Edie Brickell
- "But oh how our dreams went bump in the night and the voices downstairs getting into a fight," from "Only a Dream" (1992) by Mary Chapin Carpenter
- "Is it too much to demand/I want a full house and a rock and roll band," from "Passionate Kisses" (1992) by Lucinda Williams
- "Well you'll be cryin' for mercy when your karma/ Calls you on the phone," from "Hell to Pay" (1993) by Bonnie Raitt
- "God sometimes you just don't come through do you need a woman to look after you," from "God" (1994) by Tori Amos
- "I'm harboring a fugitive a defector of a kind she lives in my soul drinks of my wine and I'd give my last breath to keep us alive," from "Fugitive" (1994) by Amy Ray of Indigo Girls

ROCK RAP

There is magic and legend in rocks and gems. Civilizations have honored them for their beauty and thought they had healing properties. This is the language of gemstones.

MONTH	GEM	LORE
JANUARY	Garnet	Gives the wearer guidance in the night and protection from nightmares. Antidote for snakebite and food poisoning.
FEBRUARY	Amethyst	Protects from betrayal and deceit. Improves the complexion; prevents baldness.
MARCH	Aquamarine	Symbol of hope, health, and youth. Protects seafarers.
APRIL	Diamond	Symbol of love. Said to be splinters from the stars.
MAY	Emerald	Wearer can predict the future. Cures poor eyesight and low intelligence.
JUNE	Pearl	Represents wealth, honor, and longevity. Said to be heavenly dewdrops that fell into the sea.
JULY	Ruby	Said to protect from misfortune, remove evil thoughts, and make an irritable person good-tempered.
AUGUST	Peridot	Symbol of the sun. Bestows dignity and protects from evil spirits.
SEPTEMBER	Sapphire	Prevents poverty and makes a stupid person wise. Said to be sparks from the Star of Bethlehem.
OCTOBER	Opal	The stone of love and hope, said to have fallen from the sky in flashes of lightning. Renders the wearer invisible to danger.
NOVEMBER	Topaz	Cools tempers; restores sanity; cures asthma and relieves insomnia.
DECEMBER	Turquoise	Said to bring happiness and good fortune to wearers.

WE'RE TALKING DOLLS

If only dolls could talk, they would tell us they've been around as long as people. They could tell us they've been made from every imaginable earthly object, including wishbones, eggshells, flowers, and paper. They could tell us how they have been cherished and carried and buried and named. Since dolls can't talk, let's talk about dolls.

Akuba

This is the name of an Ashanti doll. Ashanti tribeswomen, from Africa, carve a square-headed wooden doll and tuck it into their waistbands when they are pregnant. The dolls are worn as good luck charms. Mothers believe that carrying these dolls will insure healthy and beautiful children.

Apple-head dolls

Native Americans were the first to make these dolls. The doll's face is carved from a fresh apple. A stick is poked into the apple heads, then the dolls are hung to dry. When they are dry, they are dressed and decorated.

Arctic dolls

The first dolls in North America were found buried in prehistoric Aleut villages. They were carved of stone or bone and dressed in sealskin. Each boy doll had a smiling face, and each girl doll had a frown.

Association dolls

An association doll is a doll connected with an event or a person. The dolls don't necessarily look like a real person, but often they do. For example, during the first presidency in America, many people made dolls that looked like George and Martha Washington.

Bartholomew babies

These were inexpensive wooden dolls which were sold at the Bartholomew Fairs in the streets of seventeenth-century London. They were brought to America by European explorers to trade with Native Americans.

Charlotte

Charlotte was the rag doll given to Laura Ingalls for Christmas in the book *Little House in the Big Woods*. She had a face of white cloth with black button eyes. Her other features were painted with the ink of pokeberries. Her hair was made of black yarn knit into curls.

China dolls

These dolls were made from porcelain or ceramic-ware that originated in China. A china doll was often made with a china head only. The first ones in America were made with china heads imported from Europe which were then attached to cloth bodies. Peddlers sold the dolls from their wagons.

Chippewa dolls

Like most Native American tribes, the Chippewa made dolls for their daughters and their sons. Dolls were made from the bark of the slippery elm tree, cattails, pine needles, and leaves. Rag dolls were made of buckskin, stuffed with dried moss, and adorned with jewelry.

Coffin dolls

These dolls first appeared as playthings in the late

Did you know that paper cutout dolls have been around for centuries? Cutouts first appeared in eighteenth-century France and then became popular again in the United States in the twentieth century.

eighteenth century. They were made of wood and could be removed from their tiny lidded coffins.

Corn dolls
These dolls, made of cornhusks or corncobs or both, were popular among America's early settlers. The first to make corn dolls were Native Americans. The dolls' hair was most often made from the corn-silk.

Handkerchief dolls
When the American pioneers were traveling westward, children would often fashion dolls from a piece of rolled cloth. The eyes, ears, and mouth were marked in ink.

Happy heads
These were wish dolls made by Native Americans, particularly those living in the northeast and the midwest. The heads were made of apples and the bodies of cornhusks. They were symbols of good fortune.

Izannah Walker dolls
Izannah Walker of Rhode Island was, in 1873, the first person to patent a doll. She made and sold or gave away more than a thousand dolls. Her dolls were made of layers of cloth and paste and were painted with oils.

Kachina dolls
The Hopi and Zuni Indians of the Southwest make these wooden dolls to teach their children the symbols and rites of their religion. The dolls, made to represent more than 200 spirits, are replicas of costumed and masked dancers. They are often

hung from the rafters of their homes. The Hopi use the dried roots of cottonwood trees to make their dolls. The Zuni use pine trees. Zuni dolls are taller than Hopi dolls and have feet.

Kewpie dolls

In 1913, small, cupid-like dolls with chubby bodies, tiny wings, top knots, and mischievous smiles became very popular. Like many dolls today, kewpie dolls came in a range of materials and characters: cloth, porcelain, and plastic; carpenter, cook, and chieftain. People formed kewpie clubs and bought everything related to kewpie dolls: books, soap, handkerchiefs, and even saltshakers. Rose O'Neill created the kewpie doll and became a millionaire.

Molly Brinkerhoff

Molly was a doll that was buried by her owners along with their household goods when the British invaded Long Island in the days before the American Revolution. When Molly was dug up, she became a keepsake for generations of Brinkerhoffs, who associated her with that period in history.

Pennywooden dolls

These are English dolls carved out of wood. The joints are movable and fastened by pegs. These are also known as dancing dolls.

Pioneer dolls

Most pioneer dolls were small, between 3 and 10 inches high. A typical doll had a twig or pine cone body. A child doll had a chestnut head; an adult doll had a hickory head. Acorns, pecans, and walnuts were also used to make these dolls. They were made by women and children who traveled to and settled in the wilderness that became the United States, before there were ever stores that sold dolls.

Poppets
These dolls were homemade by New Englanders in the mid-nineteenth century. Poppets made of rags and hog bristles and stuffed with hair were owned by two eccentric old women in Salem, Massachusetts. Their poppets were used as evidence against them when they were tried and hanged as witches.

Raggedy Ann
In 1915, when Johnny Gruelle found an old rag doll his mother had played with as a child, he was inspired to write a story about the doll. Her most important feature was her heart. In 1918 the first Raggedy Ann doll went on sale, but was soon recalled—parents were angry that she was missing her famous heart.

> *Clarissa Field's wooden doll named Bangwell Putt was given to the Memorial Museum of Deerfield, Massachusetts, in 1882. Clarissa, who was born blind in 1765, had a great collection of dolls and an even greater list of names for them. They were: Pingo, Palica, Himonarro, Ebby Puttence, and Bangwell Putt. Bangwell Putt is one of the earliest dolls with a documented history.*

Sally
Sally is also known as the "White House doll." She is a large cloth doll with a painted face and a red and white calico dress. She lived in the White House when John Quincy Adams was president. His grandchildren loved and played with Sally.

Swartzentruber dolls
These dolls are made by a strict Amish sect. The dolls are dressed in plain clothes of blue or grey.

They have no arms or legs and are faceless. This is in keeping with the Bible's commandment to make no likeness or image of anything on earth.

Topsy-turvy dolls

These are rag dolls made with a head at each end of the body. One head is always covered up by the doll's clothes, so there are really two different dolls in one. Popular topsy-turvy dolls were inspired by storybook characters like Little Red Riding Hood  and the Wolf. Also popular were black and white dolls, with one head that was black, and one that was white.

Wishbone dolls

In the late 1800s adults saved the wishbones from turkeys and chickens and made dolls out of them using a piece of cork for the head and sealing wax for the feet. The dolls were dressed in the fashions of the time.

Worry dolls

These are tiny dolls from Guatemala. You tell one worry to each doll, place the dolls you've told the worries to under your pillow, and by the morning they've taken your troubles away.

WHAT'S YOUR SIGN?

People who believe in astrology talk about how personalities are influenced by birth signs. The zodiac is a band of stars which seem to encircle the earth. It is divided into twelve parts called signs. These are the signs of the zodiac and some of the characteristics associated with them:

AQUARIUS: January 20 to February 18.
Curious, outgoing, independent

PISCES: February 19 to March 20.
Artistic, sensitive, emotional

ARIES: March 21 to April 19.
Bold, courageous, energetic

TAURUS: April 20 to May 20.
Conservative, possessive, loyal, stubborn

GEMINI: May 21 to June 20.
Lively, talkative, intelligent

CANCER: June 21 to July 22.
Emotional, patriotic, powerful

LEO: July 23 to August 22.
Cheerful, proud, powerful

VIRGO: August 23 to September 22.
Modest, practical, tidy

LIBRA: September 23 to October 22.
Pleasant, diplomatic, companionable

SCORPIO: October 23 to November 21.
Secretive, intense, passionate

SAGITTARIUS: November 22 to December 21.
Cheerful, generous, restless

CAPRICORN: December 22 to January 19.
Ambitious, cautious, practical

WHAT'S YOUR ASTROLOGICAL MASCOT?

MASCOT	BIRTHDATES
RAVEN AND OWL	December 23 to February 19
LARK AND PHEASANT	February 20 to March 20, and November 22 to December 22
EAGLE AND HAWK	March 21 to April 20, and October 23 to November 21
MAGPIE AND PARROT	May 23 and June 21, and August 23 to September 22
SWALLOW AND DOVE	September 23 to October 22, and April 21 to May 22
DUCK	June 22 to July 22
HEN	July 23 to August 22

Invention Convention

U.S. HISTORY IS FULL OF FEMALE inventors who have been overlooked or robbed of recognition for their inventions. Women's discoveries, whether for use in the home or on the battlefield, have affected our lives. Can you imagine a car without windshield wipers? Groceries without a brown paper bag?

FEMALE INGENUITY

The following is a partial list of the many ingenious inventions by women.

INVENTION	INVENTOR	YEAR
Battery container	Nancy Perkins	1986
Beehive	Thiphena Hornbrook	1861
Canister vacuum	Nancy Perkins	1987
Car heater	Margaret Wilcox	1893
Circular saw	Tabitha Babbit	1812
Cooking stove	Elizabeth Hawk	1867
Dam and reservoir construction	Harriet Strong	1887
Direct and return mailing envelope	Beulah Henry	1962
Dishwasher	Josephine Cochran	1872
Drinking fountain device	Laurene O'Donnell	1985
Electric hot water heater	Ida Forbes	1917
Elevated railway	Mary Walton	1881
Engine muffler	El Dorado Jones	1917
Feedback control for data processing	Erna Hoover	1971
Fire escape	Anna Connelly	1887
Globes	Ellen Fitz	1875
Grain storage bin	Lizzie Dickelman	1920
Improved locomotive wheels	Mary Jane Montgomery	1864
Improvement in dredging machines	Emily Tassey	1876
Improvement in stone pavements	Emily Gross	1877
Kevlar, a steel-like fiber used in radial tires, crash helmets, and bulletproof vests	Stephanie Kwolek	1966

INVENTION	INVENTOR	YEAR
Life raft	Maria Beaseley	1882
Locomotive chimney	Mary Walton	1879
Medical syringe	Letitia Geer	1899
Mop-wringer pail	Eliza Wood	1889
Oil burner	Amanda Jones	1880
Permanent wave for the hair	Marjorie Joyner	1928
Portable screen summer house	Nettie Rood	1882
Refrigerator	Florence Parpart	1914
Rolling pin	Catherine Deiner	1891
Rotary engine	Margaret Knight	1904
Safety device for elevators	Harriet Tracy	1892
Street cleaning machine	Florence Parpart	1900
Submarine lamp and telescope	Sara Mather	1870
Suspenders	Laura Cooney	1896
Washing machine	Margaret Colvin	1871
Windshield wiper	Mary Anderson	1903
Zigzag sewing machine	Helen Blanchard	1873

UNCONVENTIONAL INVENTORS

These women achieved fame through their talent as actors, artists, and entertainers. They also were talented inventors who all earned patents for their inventions.

Mary Cassatt was a famous painter who, during World War I, invented a hammock for a fractured leg, an appliance for a fractured arm, and a splint for an injured wrist. All these inventions were created to help the war wounded.

Lillian Russell invented a combination dresser-trunk that she used on theatrical tours. She was a stage actor who needed to transport her makeup and costumes when on tour.

May Robson was an actor who invented a false leg for stage use.

Hedy Lamar was a movie actor who invented a secret communications system for use by the War Department against the Nazis. After the patent had expired, however, a large U.S. corporation developed a similar system and sold it to the government.

MOTHERS OF INVENTION

They say necessity is the mother of invention. But mothers are the mothers of these inventions for kids.

INVENTION	INVENTOR	YEAR
Alphabet blocks	Adeline Whitney	1882
Ansa baby bottle	Nickie Campbell	1984
Baby jumper	Jane Wells	1872
Barney (the purple dinosaur)	Sheryl Leach	1988
Careerpals dolls	Linda Stockdale	1991
Diapers	Maria Allen	1887
Disposable diapers	Marion Donovan	1951
Flexible kite	Gertrude Rogallo	1951
Folding crib	Sarah Neal	1894
Infant carrier (Snugli)	Agnes Auckerman & Ann Moore	1962
Movable doll eyes	Beulah Henry	1935
School desk	Anna Breadin	1889
Zoothbrush (easy to grasp, fanciful toothbrushes)	Susan Harrison	1993

WHEN FOOD FIRES THE IMAGINATION

- Nancy Johnson invented the ice cream freezer in 1843.
- In 1893, Sara Tyson Rorer suggested to the Knox Gelatin Company that they add sparkling granulated sugar to gelatin, and Jell-O was born.
- Amanda Jones invented fruit bars, improvements in preserving fruits and vegetables, and the vacuum method of canning foods, all in the 1860s.

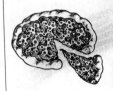

- Minnie Phelps invented a combined toaster and warming oven in 1906.
- Madeline Turner invented a machine for extracting juice from fruit in 1916.
- Ruth Wakefield invented the chocolate chip cookie in 1933. She named her creations "tollhouse cookies" after the Tollhouse restaurant she owned in Massachusetts because it was there that she created the cookies.

- Ruth Siems developed Stove Top Stuffing while working for General Foods Corporation in 1975.
- Virginia Holsinger invented Lactaid, a low-lactose dairy product used by people who cannot digest milk, in 1976.

- Rose Totino patented a dough for frozen pizza in 1979.
- Heida Thurlow patented the covered frying pan and the food warming stand in the late 1980s.
- Penny Cooper invented a plastic pouch to hold dehydrated food in 1985.
- Lynn Deffenbaugh invented a frozen food package for use in the microwave oven in 1987.

BRAIN CHILD

A brain child is an original idea. Here are some kids who had great ideas which they turned into inventions. We call these kids "brain children."

- Six-year-old Suzanna Goodin, tired of cleaning the cat food spoon, came up with the idea of an edible spoon-shaped cracker. She won a grand prize for her invention in the Weekly Reader National Invention Contest.

- Eight-year-old Theresa Thompson and her nine-year-old sister Mary were the youngest sisters to receive a U.S. patent. They invented a solar tepee for a science fair project in 1960. They called the device a Wigwarm.

Two inspirational books for girl inventors are Elsie's Invention *by Mary Mapes Dodge, and* The Big Balloon Race *by Eleanor Coerr.*

- At the age of nine, Margaret Knight began working in a cotton mill, where she saw a steel-tipped shuttle fly out of a loom and hit a nearby worker. As a result, Margaret devised her first invention: a shuttle restraining device. She went on to invent the machine that makes the square-bottom paper bags we still use for groceries today. That machine was patented in 1871.

- Eleven-year-old Jeanie Low became the youngest female on record to receive a patent on March 10, 1992. She invented the Kiddie Stool—a foldup stool that fits under the sink so kids can unfold it, stand on it, and reach the sink on their own!

- Becky Schroeder began her patenting career when she was 14 years old. She put phosphorescent paint on paper under her writing paper so that she could write in the dark. This invention was later used in all sorts of ways. Doctors use it in hospitals to read patients' charts at night without waking them, and astronauts use it

BRAIN CHILD

A brain child is an original idea. Here are some kids who had great ideas which they turned into inventions. We call these kids "brain children."

- Six-year-old Suzanna Goodin, tired of cleaning the cat food spoon, came up with the idea of an edible spoon-shaped cracker. She won a grand prize for her invention in the Weekly Reader National Invention Contest.

- Eight-year-old Theresa Thompson and her nine-year-old sister Mary were the youngest sisters to receive a U.S. patent. They invented a solar tepee for a science fair project in 1960. They called the device a Wigwarm.

- At the age of nine, Margaret Knight began working in a cotton mill, where she saw a steel-tipped shuttle fly out of a loom and hit a nearby worker. As a result, Margaret devised her first invention: a shuttle restraining device. She went on to invent the machine that makes the square-bottom paper bags we still use for groceries today. That machine was patented in 1871.

- Eleven-year-old Jeanie Low became the youngest female on record to receive a patent on March 10, 1992. She invented the Kiddie Stool—a foldup stool that fits under the sink so kids can unfold it, stand on it, and reach the sink on their own!

- Becky Schroeder began her patenting career when she was 14 years old. She put phosphorescent paint on paper under her writing paper so that she could write in the dark. This invention was later used in all sorts of ways. Doctors use it in hospitals to read patients' charts at night without waking them, and astronauts use it

Two inspirational books for girl inventors are Elsie's Invention *by Mary Mapes Dodge, and* The Big Balloon Race *by Eleanor Coerr.*

WHEN FOOD FIRES THE IMAGINATION

- Nancy Johnson invented the ice cream freezer in 1843.

- In 1893, Sara Tyson Rorer suggested to the Knox Gelatin Company that they add sparkling granulated sugar to gelatin, and Jell-O was born.

- Amanda Jones invented fruit bars, improvements in preserving fruits and vegetables, and the vacuum method of canning foods, all in the 1860s.

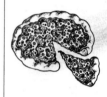

- Minnie Phelps invented a combined toaster and warming oven in 1906.

- Madeline Turner invented a machine for extracting juice from fruit in 1916.

- Ruth Wakefield invented the chocolate chip cookie in 1933. She named her creations "tollhouse cookies" after the Tollhouse restaurant she owned in Massachusetts because it was there that she created the cookies.

- Ruth Siems developed Stove Top Stuffing while working for General Foods Corporation in 1975.

- Virginia Holsinger invented Lactaid, a low-lactose dairy product used by people who cannot digest milk, in 1976.

- Rose Totino patented a dough for frozen pizza in 1979.

- Heida Thurlow patented the covered frying pan and the food warming stand in the late 1980s.

- Penny Cooper invented a plastic pouch to hold dehydrated food in 1985.

- Lynn Deffenbaugh invented a frozen food package for use in the microwave oven in 1987.

when their electrical systems are turned down for recharging.

- 14-year-old Pamela Sica invented a push-button device that raises the floor of a car so that cargo can be raised and easily removed. Her invention won a grand prize for her age group in the Weekly Reader National Invention Contest. She wanted to patent her invention but found that it was too expensive.

FRIBBLES

Here are some inventions that seemed frivolous, strange, or humorous to us. What do you think? Would you call them fribbles, too?

- A combination butter churn and clothes washer was patented by Mary Bridges in 1883.

- A mustache guard to attach to spoons or cups to keep a mustache dry while eating soups or drinking liquids was invented by Mary Evans in 1899.

- A diaper for parakeets was invented by Bertha Lugi in 1959.

- The spaghetti cinch patented by Dicksie Spolar shows precisely how much spaghetti to cook to yield up to 10 servings.

- A lip-shaping device for women was invent-

The United States patent laws protect your inventions in several ways:

- **Utility patents.** These are seventeen-year patents granted to protect "new, useful and not obvious processes, machines, compositions of matter and articles of manufacture."

- **Design patents.** These are fourteen-year patents granted to anyone who has invented a new, original, or ornamental design for something.

- **Plant patents.** These are seventeen-year patents granted to protect the creation of new varieties of plants. The plants must be reproduced "by means other than seeds, such as by rooting of cuttings, or by grafting."

- **Trademark.** This method of protecting your invention refers to a wide variety of commercial marks. The trademark can be a word, name, symbol, or device used by a manufacturer or seller to identify their product.

- **Trade secrets.** These are secret formulas, patterns, devices, or data used in a business that give that business an edge over its competition. Trade secrets are not published like patents, so the technology cannot be studied by others. State laws protect trade secrets.

The first female patent examiner was Ann Nichols of Massachusetts. She became an examiner in 1873.

ed by Hazel Mann. It consisted of a pair of hard rubber lips attached to a handle. The device was applied to a woman's lips, the handle was squeezed, and the lips were pinched and re-shaped into the lip style fashionable in the 1920s.

- A Cheeky Derriere Relief was invented by Julie Newmar in 1975. It was a body-shaping panty-hose or tights that pushed the wearer's buttocks up. The inventor called it "body perfecting hose."
- A dress elevator, a device to lift long dresses off the ground, was invented by Ellen Demorest in 1880.
- The Rocking Chair Fan Attachment was invented by Mary Ann Woodward in 1849.

CAMPS, CONTESTS, AND PURSUING A PATENT

The following is a list of places to visit, camps to attend, and contests to enter. Have fun!

How to get a patent

If you think you have a great invention and want to have it patented, you need a great deal of determination and money. Your idea must be explained clearly to a patent examiner to determine whether it is new and useful. You must have an illustration of the device in action. Many people hire patent attorneys to be sure their patents conform to U.S. Patent Office rules. If you get a patent, your invention will have a number and you alone will have the right to sell your device. For more information, call the U.S. Patent and Trademark Office at (703) 557-7800 or write OEIPS, P.O. Box 9, Washington, D.C. 20231.

Invention contest

Weekly Reader, a classroom magazine, sponsors a national invention contest every year. Grand prizes include savings bonds and a trip to the National Inventor's Exposition at the U.S. Patent Office, where the winners' inventions are exhibited.

National Inventors Hall of Fame

The National Inventors' Hall of Fame was founded in 1973 and is dedicated to U.S. patent holders whose inventions have made great technological advances. It is located at the National Invention Center, 80 West Bowery Street, Akron, Ohio.

Camps

- *Camp Invention.* In 1993 more than 1,500 children developed their creative abilities at Camp Invention during summer vacation. The camp is for anyone in grades 1 through 6, and camps are held at 16 sites in 12 states.
- *Camp Ingenuity* is for girls in grades 7 through 9. For more information about both camps call (216) 762-4463.
- *U.S. Space Camps* are located in Florida and Alabama. In Alabama, the camp is for students in grades 4 through 6. In Florida, the camp is for students in grades 4 through 7. The Florida site is located at the entrance to NASA's launch complex. At both camps you learn what it takes to become an astronaut. During the week-long session, you become familiar with the U.S. Space Transportation System and participate in simulated shuttle missions.
- *U.S. Space Academy* is located in Alabama and

In 1991 Gertrude Elion became the first woman inducted into the Inventors' Hall of Fame. She invented drugs to treat gout, leukemia, and organ transplant rejection.

One of America's most successful inventors was Madame C. J. Walker. She invented hair care products for African Americans, which she began selling door to door in 1905. Over time she built a huge cosmetics and hair products empire and became the first African American millionaire in the U.S.

is for students in grades 7 through 9. At the U.S. Space Academy, participants are given specialized learning opportunities not available in Space Camp. There is extra emphasis on space shuttle operations and mission training.

For information write:

in Alabama
U.S. Space Camp or U.S. Space Academy
P.O. Box 070015
Huntsville, Alabama 35807-7015

in Florida
U.S. Space Camp
6225 Vectorpace Blvd.
Titusville, Florida 32780

NINE NOBEL PRIZE WINNERS
IN SCIENCE

Marie Sklodowska Curie
(Physics, 1903 and Chemistry, 1911)
Marie Curie is considered the most famous of all women scientists. She was the only person ever to win two Nobel Prizes. By the time she was 16, Marie had already won a gold medal at the Russian lycée in Poland upon the completion of her secondary education. In 1891, almost penniless, she began her education at the Sorbonne in Paris. In 1903 her discovery of radioactivity earned her the Nobel Prize in physics. In 1911 she won it for chemistry.

MARIE CURIE

Irene Curie (Chemistry, 1933)
Irene Curie was the daughter of Marie Curie. She furthered her mother's work in radioactivity and won the Nobel Prize for discovering that radioactivity could be artificially produced.

Gerty Radnitz Cori (Biochemistry, 1947)
Gerty Cori was the first American woman to win a Nobel Prize in science. She studied enzymes and hormones, and her work brought researchers closer to understanding diabetes. She won the Nobel Prize for discovering the enzymes that convert glycogen into sugar and back again to glycogen.

Barbara McClintock (Medicine, 1983)
Barbara McClintock studied the chromosomes in corn/maize and her work uncovered antibiotic-resistant bacteria and a possible cure for African sleeping sickness.

Maria Goeppert Mayer (Physics, 1963)
Maria researched the structure of atomic nuclei. During World War II she worked on isotope separation for the atomic bomb project.

Rita Levi-Montalicini (Medicine, 1986)
Rita is an Italian neuroembryologist known for her codiscovery in 1954 of nerve growth factor, a previously unknown protein that stimulates the growth of nerve cells and plays a role in degenerative diseases like Alzheimer's disease. She received the Nobel Prize in Medicine in 1986.

Dorothy Crowfoot Hodgkin (Chemistry, 1964)
Dorothy discovered the structures of penicillin and vitamin B_{12}. She won the Nobel Prize for determining the structure of biochemical compounds essential to combating pernicious anemia.

Gertrude Elion (Medicine, 1988)
Gertrude Elion is the only woman inventor inducted into The Inventors Hall of Fame. She invented the leukemia-fighting drug 6-mercaptopurine. Her continued research led to Imuran, a derivative of 6-mercaptopurine that blocks the body's rejection of foreign tissues.

Rosalyn Sussman Yalow (Medicine, 1977)
Rosayln Yalow won the Nobel Prize for developing radioimmunoassay, a test of body tissues that uses radioactive isotopes to measure the concentrations of hormones, viruses, vitamins, enzymes, and drugs.

DISEASE FIGHTERS

AIDS
In 1988 a team of researchers led by the chemist Jane Rideout won a patent for AZT, a drug used to fight AIDS, aquired immune deficiency syndrome.

Apnea
Mary Horn, a researcher and pediatric nurse, developed the Apnea Detection Device to combat sudden infant death syndrome. It is attached to a sleeping baby to monitor the baby's breathing. If the baby stops breathing, an alarm goes off.

Apgar tests
Virginia Apgar created the now internationally used Apgar Score, which evaluates a baby's overall condition within one minute of birth.

Cystic fibrosis
Dorothy Hansine Anderson was the first to identify cystic fibrosis. She devised an easy method of diagnosing the disease in its early stages.

Meningitis
Hattie Elizabeth Alexander developed the meningitis serum. Before her discovery this disease was 100 percent fatal in infants.

Fungicide
Rachel Brown and Elizabeth Hazen discovered the antibiotic nystatin in 1948. Nystatin was the first safe fungicide, and was considered the greatest biomedical breakthrough since the 1928 discovery of penicillin. Nystatin is used to cure a wide variety of ailments, including athlete's foot.

Rickets
Martha Eliot was a codeveloper of the cure for rickets, a disease that causes defective bone growth. The cure is cod liver oil and lots of sunshine.

Cancer
Gladys Anderson Emerson isolated vitamin E from wheat germ oil. Her research led to greater understanding of the link between cancer and nutrition.

Brucellosis
Alice Evans discovered the cause of the deadly disease brucellosis, or undulant fever. The cause of this disease was contaminated milk.

Mononucleosis
Karen Elizabeth Willard-Gallo invented and patented a method for early detection of infectious mononucleosis.

Polio
Dr. Dorothy Horstman identified the polio virus in its early stages. Her discovery was an important factor in developing a vaccine.

Rheumatic fever
Rebecca Lancefield is credited with first categorizing the organism responsible for rheumatic fever.

Hodgkin's disease
Dorothy Mendenhall identified the cell that causes Hodgkin's disease.

Sleeping sickness
Louise Pearce was the coinventor of the serum that cures sleeping sickness.

Making Connections

FRIEND-TO-FRIEND, SISTER-TO-
sister, mother-to-daughter, all are
 strong relation-
ships. Whether
connections are
based on blood or bonding, they
can be enduring. Take a look at
these
famous
female
connec-
tions.

SISTER ACTS

Throughout history there have been feuding sisters, singing sisters, writing sisters, even hidden sisters. Some are famous, some are forgotten. Here are some stories from the sister connection file.

Singing Sisters

- The Andrews Sisters, Patti, Maxene, and LaVerne, were a popular singing trio in the 1940s. They started singing to keep from quarreling. Two of their hit songs, "Beer Barrel Polka" and "Boogie Woogie Bugle Boy," helped to make their lifetime record sales top 60 million.
- The Boswell Sisters, Connee, Martha, and Helvetia, sang and accompanied themselves on piano, guitar, violin, and banjo. Their most popular recording was their 1930s version of "You Ought to Be in Pictures."
- Heart, a hard rock band, features sisters Nancy and Ann Wilson. They hit the charts in the 1980s with songs like "Crazy on You."
- The Hyer Sisters were Anna and Emma, the first black women performers to tour after the Civil War. Anna was a soprano and Emma was a contralto. Together they formed a popular singing duo with a versatile repertoire which included arias, ballads, and plantation songs.
- The King Sisters were a vocal group popular in the big band era of the 1930s. Donna, Louise, Alyce, and Yvonne King renewed their popularity in the mid 1960s with a television show, *The King Family*.
- The Lennon Sisters, Peggy, Kathy, Janet, and Diane, became a regular and popular feature of

"The sisterhood is powerful" is a slogan coined by Kathie Sarachild. She wrote the words in a leaflet that was distributed during the Burial of Traditional Womanhood demonstration in Washington, D.C., in 1968.

the musical entertainment TV program, *The Lawrence Welk Show.*

- The McGuire Sisters were a popular singing trio in the 1950s. Dorothy, Phyllis, and Christine are best remembered for their hit "Sincerely."
- The Pointer Sisters, Ruth, Anita, Bonnie, and June, were songwriters and singers who emerged in the 1970s wearing sassy costumes and singing pop, rock, and country and western. One of their hits was "I'm So Excited."

Solo Sisters

- Country music singers Loretta Lynn and Crystal Gale are sisters.
- Pop singer Janet Jackson is sister to singer La-Toya Jackson.

Script Sisters

- The Brontë sisters, Anne, Charlotte, and Emily, were all published authors. Their mother died a year after the youngest, Anne, was born, so the three sisters were raised by their aunt, Elizabeth Branwell. They spent most of their lives isolated on the English moors. Their first published work was a book of poems using the pen names Currer (for Charlotte), Ellis (for Emily) and Acton (for Anne) Bell. Using their own names, Emily authored *Wuthering Heights,* Anne wrote *Agnes Grey,* and Charlotte wrote *Jane Eyre.* Charlotte's success with her book was saddened by the deaths of her two sisters within a year of its 1847 publication.
- The Delaney sisters, Sarah ("Sadie") and Annie Elizabeth ("Bessie"), wrote their memoir, *Having Our Say: The Delaney Sisters' First Hundred*

Years, when they were 103 and 101 years old, respectively. They were the daughters of slaves and they went on to distinguish themselves in professional occupations. Bessie was the second black female dentist in New York state. Sadie became the first black home economics teacher in a New York City high school. Their secrets to long life include yoga, cod liver oil, and a daily dose of fresh garlic.

- Ann Landers and Abigail Van Buren are twin sisters who write advice columns for newspapers. Originally Ann was named Esther Pauline and Abby was named Pauline Esther. Ann was the first to write an advice column; one year later Abigail got her start. Both are very successful, and they are still close.

- Louisa May Alcott, the author of *Little Women,* had three sisters, Anna, Elizabeth, and May. The characters in *Little Women* were based on her sisters. Louisa was most like Jo, the feisty one; Meg was the pretty one; Beth was musical and fragile; and Amy was vain. Louisa supported her family and sisters with her writing. She published 270 works.

SECRET SISTERS

These are sisters who most people don't know... they've been hidden by history or the fame of their siblings.

Agatha Christie, the prolific writer of mystery stories, wrote her first novel as a response to her sister's challenge. When asked if she could write an irresistible detective story, Agatha responded with *The Mysterious Affair at Styles,* the first of 90 books that sold over 400 million copies and were translated into 103 languages.

The American poet Emily Dickinson had a sister named Lavinia who also lived at home and, like Emily, rarely left the house. During Emily's lifetime only seven of her poems were published, but after her death Lavinia discovered hundreds more tucked into secret places throughout the house. Thanks to Lavinia, all of Emily's poems were finally published.

Judy Garland, the singer and actor best remembered for her role as Dorothy in *The Wizard of Oz,* started her show business career singing with The Gumm Sisters. She was "Baby Frances," and with her two older sisters, Mary Jane and Virginia, she sang on the vaudeville circuit. When she went solo at the age of seven, she took the name Judy from her favorite song, also called "Judy," and added Garland because it sounded better than her real last name, Gumm.

Joan Fisher, the older sister of Bobby Fisher, the first American world chess champion, was also his babysitter. When he was 6 and she was 11, she watched him after school, on weekends, and during vacations. She frequently played board games with him. One afternoon in 1949 Joan bought a chess set at a local candy store in Brooklyn, brought it home, and taught Bobby how to play. She was the hidden sister who helped produce a champion.

Anne Frank will always be remembered for her

book *The Diary of a Young Girl,* but how many remember that Anne had an older sister, Margot, who lived in hiding from the Nazis with her and suffered the same death in a concentration camp? In her diary, Anne expressed the kind of jealousy that is typical between sisters when she wrote that her parents, especially her mother, preferred Margot to her. Margot had the better grades and was well liked by adults. Anne also felt that Peeter Van Daans, who hid with them, had a crush on Margot. Both Anne and Margot died of typhus in the concentration camp at Bergen-Belsen in Germany.

Aretha Franklin, the "Queen of Soul," has a talented sister named Irma. Irma Franklin is a songwriter whose best-known work, "Piece of my Heart," was recorded by Janis Joplin. Other songs by Irma have been recorded by her sister, Aretha.

Although Fanny Mendelssohn was a gifted musician and composer, she spent most of her life acting as a music consultant to her famous younger brother, Felix. Both her father and her brother disapproved of women performing in public or publishing, so Fanny remained the hidden sister. The Mendelssohn family lived in Germany in the early 1800s, but Felix Mendelssohn's music is still performed by classical musicians today.

Wolfgang Mozart was a child prodigy. So was his older sister Nannerl. Their father taught them both how to play the clavier, a keyboard instrument, as soon as they could sit up. Nannerl and Wolfgang began performing at the ages of 10 and 5, respectively, for the royal courts of Europe, where they were showered with gifts of gold and silver coins for their sensational performances. Wolfgang went on to compose the music for which he is so well remembered.

Dorothy Wordsworth and her brother, William, grew up in the lovely Lake District of England. The landscape provided inspiration for William Wordsworth's poetry. Another inspiration for William was his sister's writings. Although Dorothy was not published, her journals and letters show that William frequently borrowed her lyrical comments on nature and the rustic people who roamed the countryside.

ALL IN THE FAMILY

HARRIET BEECHER STOWE

- *Harriet and Catharine Beecher.* Harriet Beecher Stowe was the author of *Uncle Tom's Cabin.* Catharine Beecher was a notable educator who worked for advanced education for women. She also founded and headed the Hartford Seminary for Girls.

- *Elizabeth and Emily Blackwell.* Elizabeth was the first woman doctor in the U.S. Emily was also a physician. Together the sisters founded the New York Infirmary for Women and Children in 1868.

- *Nadia and Lili Boulanger.* Nadia was the first female to conduct the Boston Symphony Orchestra (1939). Lili was a composer who died young, at the age of 24, leaving more than 50 musical compositions as her legacy.

- *Joan and Jackie Collins.* Joan Collins is a TV

actor. Jackie is the author of popular fiction.

- *Eva, Zsa Zsa, and Madgda Gabor.* These sisters are all actors and media personalities.
- *Sarah and Angelina Grimké.* These sisters shared antislavery careers. In 1830 they were the first women lecturers of the American Anti-Slavery Society.
- *Emma and Josephine Lazarus.* Emma was a poet, best known for "The New Collosus," which is inscribed on the base of the Statue of Liberty. Josephine was a social worker who devoted her life to helping immigrants in America.
- *Lynn and Vanessa Redgrave.* These British sisters are both actors.
- *Soon Ai-ling and Mai-ling.* These are the celebrated Soon sisters of China. Soon Mai-ling became the powerful Madame Chiang Kai-shek. Soon Ai-ling was a famous social worker.
- *Joan Fontaine and Olivia de Havilland.* These sisters are actors.
- *Tia and Tamera Mowry.* These twin sisters have modeled and acted in commercials since childhood. In 1994 they turned 16 and started an acting career on the TV show "Sister, Sister."

LIKE MOTHER, LIKE DAUGHTER
These women have followed in their mothers' footsteps:

Printers:
- Sarah Goddard was a printer in colonial America. Her daughter Katherine was the first to print the Declaration of Independence.

"In search of my mother's garden, I found my own."
—Alice Walker

Feminists:

- Lucy Stone, one of the leaders of the nineteenth century women's suffrage movement had a daughter, Alice Stone Blackwell (Blackwell was her father's name). Alice was also a feminist and very active in the women's rights movement.
- Elizabeth Cady Stanton's daughter, Harriet Stanton Blatch, organized the Equality League of Self-Supporting Women in 1907. Elizabeth was one of the leaders of the mid-nineteenth century women's movement.

Bandits:

- Belle Starr was dubbed the "Bandit Queen" of the Wild West. She was an outlaw who was killed under mysterious circumstances. Her daughter, Pearl, also became an outlaw.

Scientists:

- Both Marie Curie and her daughter Irene Joliot-Curie were Nobel Prize–winning physicists.

Soldiers:

- Leola Hopkins was the first woman to enlist in the U.S. Navy after the outbreak of World War II. Her mother was a corporal in the female Marine reserve unit during World War I.

Performers:

- Liza Minelli is a performer who sings and dances. Her mother, Judy Garland, was a singer, dancer, and actor.
- Maybelle Carter was an original member of the Carter Family, an American country and folk singing group. After the group broke up, Maybelle and her daughters, June, Anita, and Helen,

Nowadays, the nickname "Lucy Stoner" is given to women who keep their own last names after marrying.

became regulars at the Grand Ole Opry in Nashville, Tennessee. Later, "Mother" Maybelle and her daughters founded a country music dynasty.

- Michelle Phillips was a member of the '70s singing group The Mamas and the Papas. Her daughter Chynna Phillips was recently a singer in the popular trio Wilson Phillips.
- Keisha Jackson started singing backup for her mother, soul singer Millie Jackson, at the age of 15. She then struck out on her own, recording two successful albums by 1994.

Authors:

- Hilma Wolitzer started writing fiction at the kitchen table with her kids and her dogs around her. One of those kids, her daughter Meg, published her first novel, *Friends for Life,* in 1994, at the same time her mother published her novel *Tunnel of Love.* They went on a seven-city promotional tour together.

BEST FRIENDS

True friends are loyal, trusting, and have shared interests. True friends have fun together. Here are some well-known women who were true friends.

Anne Sullivan met Helen Keller when she was hired to teach her. Anne was 20, Helen was 7. In 1904 Helen wrote *The Story of My Life,* in which she said that Anne Sullivan transformed her from an angry child into the best-educated blind and deaf person in the world. Their teacher-student relationship evolved into true friendship. They lived together for 49 years, until Sullivan died in 1936.

Did you know that Sassy *magazine is the "daughter" of* Ms. *magazine? They are published by the same company.*

Stay Connected

If you would like to read some great stories about friendship, try these books:

- *Anne of Green Gables* by L. M. Montgomery. In this book, two girls, Anne Shirley and Diana Barry, become strong friends.

- *Rebecca of Sunnybrook Farm* by Kate Douglas Wiggin tells the story of a friendship between Rebecca Randall and Emma Jane Perkins.

- The stories of Betsy, Tacy, and Tib by Maude Hart Lovelace chronicle the friendship of Betsy Ray, Tacy Kelly, and Tib Muller from when they are little girls through their high school years, and up until Betsy marries.

Riot Grrrls are activist girls in their teens and twenties who are feminists and grunge music fans. They communicate with other riot grrrls across the country through zines or fanzines—self-published, photocopied underground magazines.

Gertrude Stein's first commercial success was her book *The Autobiography of Alice B. Toklas*. Alice B. Toklas was Stein's best friend for nearly forty years. In the book Stein describes how Toklas was her proofreader, screener of visitors (of which she had many), and confidante. Alice was also Gertrude's nurse when she became ill and died in 1946.

When feminists Elizabeth Cady Stanton and Susan B. Anthony met in 1851, they became close friends. Working for the same cause, women's rights, they thought alike, worked together, and became the bedrock of the women's suffrage movement.

Anne Bonny and Mary Read were pirates and best friends. They met when Mary was captured and taken aboard Ann's pirate ship. Both had been disguised as men, but when they discovered they were both masquerading, they became inseparable friends. They were captured and tried as pirates in 1720. We don't know what happened to Ann Bonny, but Mary Read died of a fever in prison.

ORGANIZATIONS FOR GIRLS

Girl's Inc.

30 East 33rd Street, New York, NY 10016, (212) 689-3700
This is a national research and advocacy group that offers girls classes in math, science, and sex education.

Girl Scouts of U.S.A.

420 Fifth Avenue, New York, NY 10018-2702

YWCA (Young Women's Christian Association)

716 Broadway, New York, NY 10003
Offers classes in dance, yoga, swimming, and the arts.

YWHA (Young Women's Hebrew Association)

15 East 26th Street, New York, NY 10010

Ms. Foundation for Women

141 5th Avenue, New York, NY 10010
Sponsors of Take Our Daughters to Work Day. The foundation's goals are to eliminate sex discrimination and to improve the status of women and girls in society.

Women's Sports Foundation

342 Madison Avenue, New York, NY 10173-0728
Dedicated to taking girls out of the cheerleading box and on to the playing field.

NOW (National Organization for Women)

1000 16th Street, N.W., Washington, D.C. 20036
The largest women's rights organization in the U.S., NOW is dedicated to bringing women into the mainstream of American society.

FUTURE (Females Unifying Teens to Undertake Responsible Education)

This is a group formed by young women in San Leandro, California. They surveyed 400 teens in the San Francisco area and found their 5 top concerns were stress, sexuality, sexual assault, suicide, and pregnancy.

Visit the National Women's Hall of Fame in Seneca Falls, New York, where mothers, daughters, and the sisterhood are honored and recognized.

Name Calling

HAVE YOU HEARD THE QUES-
tion, *What's in a name?* Feminist Elizabeth Cady Stanton had an an-
swer: "There is a great deal in
a name.... The custom of calling a woman Mrs. John This and
Mrs. Tom That... is founded on the
principle that men are lords of all.
I cannot acknowledge this
principle as just; therefore, I
cannot bear the name of an-
other." There is a lot to be said about
names. Let's see what *is* in a name.

CODE NAME?

Do you know what your mother's name was before she married? This is known as her maiden name. Traditionally, women in America and in most European countries have taken their husband's last name when they married. So, upon marrying John Smith, Jane Doe became Jane Smith. Doe is Jane's maiden name. It is still common for banks and credit card companies to ask for your mother's maiden name and use it as a kind of identification code.

As recently as the 1960s many women in the U.S. began to use hyphens to connect their last name to their husband's last name when they got married. Others simply added their husband's name to their own, like First Lady Hillary Rodham Clinton. Still others, like Lucy Stone, kept their own names after marriage.

In China, children received their secret soul name when they ate their first dish of rice. It was called a rice name.

In Spain and Portugal it is the custom for women to add their husband's last name to their own with *y,* which means "and." So Rosa Lopez marries Juan Garcia and becomes Rosa Lopez y Garcia.

Lucy Stone was a feminist and social reformer in the nineteenth century who was one of the first and most prominent women to keep her maiden name. In 1969 a Lucy Stone League was founded for women who objected to being called by their husbands' names, like "Mrs. John Smith."

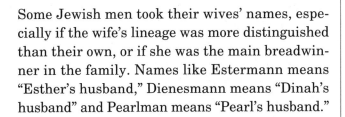

Some Jewish men took their wives' names, especially if the wife's lineage was more distinguished than their own, or if she was the main breadwinner in the family. Names like Estermann means "Esther's husband," Dienesmann means "Dinah's husband" and Pearlman means "Pearl's husband."

In Iceland, the last name of a daughter was formed by attaching the daughter's name to her father's name. Vigdis Finnbogadóttir (who was the first woman president of Iceland) means "Vigdis, the daughter of Finnboga."

Teknonymy is the tribal practice of naming the parents after their first-born child. If a child is named Soa, the mother is called Mother of Soa and the father, Father of Soa. This practice is found in Australia and Melanesia.

NICKNAMES
The Romans were the first to use nicknames. Nicknames are names that are given out of affection or given as jokes. Here are some famous nicknames.

America's First Libber
Susan B. Anthony was the leader of the women's suffrage movement.

Bloody Mary
Queen Mary I (1553–1558) was the Catholic queen of England whose persecution of Protestants earned her her nickname.

Calamity Jane
Martha Jane Cannary (1852–1903) was given this nickname because she bragged about her wild ex-

ploits as a pony express rider.

Iron Lady
Margaret Thatcher, former prime minister of
Great Britain, was given this nickname for her
strong will.

Lemonade Lucy
Lucy Hayes (1831–1889) was the wife of President
Rutherford B. Hayes and was given this name be-
cause she did not serve alcohol in the White House.

Moses
Harriet Tubman (1820–
1913) earned this nick-
name because, just as
Moses led his people out
of Egypt to the promised
land in the Bible, she
led black slaves out of
the American South to
freedom in the North.

Pocahontas
Pocahontas (1595–1617) was actually the nick-
name of the Native American princess Matoaka.
Pocahontas means "playful."

Unsinkable Molly Brown
Molly Brown (1867–1937) received nationwide
acclaim for her heroism aboard the sinking ship *Ti-
tanic* in 1912. With pistol in hand, she enforced the
sea's tradition of women and children first, organized the rowers, and helped the injured. When the
press asked how she survived, she answered "I'm
unsinkable," and it stuck as her nickname.

IXNAY TO THESE NAMES

There are many names in the English language that exclude females. Take a look at this list of exclusionary words and their nonexclusionary alternatives.

EXCLUSIONARY	NONEXCLUSIONARY
Adman	Ad writer
Brotherhood of man	Humankind, human family
Caveman	Cave dweller
Chairman	Chair, chairperson
Cleaning lady	House cleaner
Common man	Human, common citizen
Cover girl	Cover model
Fatherland	Homeland
Fisherman	Fisher
Forefather	Ancestor
Foreman	Supervisor
Founding fathers	Founders
Leading lady	Lead
Mailman	Mail carrier, postal worker
Man about town	Worldly person
Man in the street	Average person
Mankind	Humankind, humanity
Man-made	Artificial
Manpower	Work force, employees
Manpowered	Human powered, people powered
Old maids (popcorn)	No-pops, unpopped corn
Old wives' tale	Superstition, folktale
Policeman	Police officer
Showgirl	Performer, dancer
Waterboy	Water carrier
Weatherman	Weather forecaster, meteorologist

In 1984 the Minnesota State Legislature ordered that all gender-specific language be removed from the state laws. After two years of work, the rewritten laws were adopted. Only 301 of 20,000 pronouns were feminine. "His" was changed 10,000 times and "he" was changed 6,000 times.

181

WORD WATCHERS

Watch your words by calling something what it is. Name endings with -ess or -ette often carry a sense of cuteness or littleness or of being lesser versions of their male counterparts. A poet is a poet whether male or female, and a female poet should not be called a poetess. The list that follows contains non-gendered words that should be used instead of their gendered equivalents:

"Don't ever call me a jockette."
—Robyn Smith, American jockey

NO GENDER	GENDER
ACTOR	ACTRESS
AUTHOR	AUTHORESS
AVIATOR	AVIATRIX
COMEDIAN	COMEDIENNE
DRUM MAJOR	DRUM MAJORETTE
ENCHANTER	ENCHANTRESS
HEIR	HEIRESS
HERO	HEROINE
HOST	HOSTESS
LAUNDERER	LAUNDRESS
POET	POETESS
SINGER	SONGSTRESS
SORCERER	SORCERESS
STAR	STARLET
USHER	USHERETTE
WAITER	WAITRESS

A nurse is a nurse; a man is not called a male nurse.

SQUARING OFF

When addressing or writing about people of both sexes, equivalent terms must be used. For example, "man" and "wife" are not squared-off or equivalent terms, but "man" and "woman" are. Here is a list of other squared-off terms:

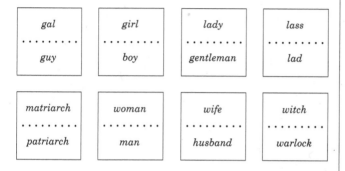

gal · · · · · · · · *guy*	*girl* · · · · · · · · *boy*	*lady* · · · · · · · · *gentleman*	*lass* · · · · · · · · *lad*
matriarch · · · · · · · · *patriarch*	*woman* · · · · · · · · *man*	*wife* · · · · · · · · *husband*	*witch* · · · · · · · · *warlock*

Have You Ever Wondered?

- Why is nature referred to as Mother Nature?

- Why are battleships, boats, and cars usually referred to as "she" instead of "it"?

- Does "man-made" mean the thing was made by a male or by a human?

- Is there always a man at the receiving end of letters addressed "Dear Sir"?

- Why did females have titles of Miss and Mrs. until recently, when Ms. was created to equate with Mr.?

- What would be a new name for the card game Old Maid?

- Why is the word "bachelor" considered equivalent to the word "spinster" when the names don't really mean the same thing any more? What would happen if we substituted "single" or "unmarried" for both words?

IN A WORD, WHO ARE YOU?

Daughter, black, average, independent, friendly, gymnast, student, dancer, nerd...What is the one word you would choose to describe yourself? Here are some of the words that well-known women have chosen to describe themselves.

"Woman." In 1851, Sojourner Truth gave her famous "Ain't I a Woman" speech at the Women's Convention in Ohio.

"Kind." Martina Navratilova, tennis champion.

"Indescribable." Margaret Atwood, author.

"Eartha." The singer Eartha Kitt said that her name described her perfectly because she is "of the earth."

"Passionate, because everything is interesting." The designer Diane Von Furstenberg described herself this way.

"Busy." Eileen Ford, chairman of Ford Modeling Agency.

"Ambition" describes feminist and social critic Camille Paglia well because, as she said, "My ambition was always the development of my talent."

"Vim." Describes W. Ann Reynolds, Chancellor of City University of New York, because she is "Endeavoring to be a wife, mother, daughter, sister, aunt—once a scientist, now an educator—always a student."

"Forward." Anna Deavere Smith, actor and playwright.

"Moody." Susanna Kaysen, author.

NAME POWER

- Some Native Americans have two names, one of which is never made public because of the power it would give another person over them.

- It is common in parts of West Africa for people to name their children for the day on which they were born. Sunday is *Awushie,* Monday is *Adojoa,* Tuesday is *Abla,* Wednesday is *Aku,* Thursday is *Awo,* Friday is *Afua,* and Saturday is *Ama.*

- In seventeenth-century Europe people made anagrams from names and believed these words formed from rearranging the letters would give a clue to a person's characteristics. Teresa is a teaser, Pat is apt, Greta is great, Mona likes to moan, and Dora travels on the road.

- Names that are palindromes (spelled the same backwards and forwards) include Ava, Anna, and Hannah.

- There were tribes in the mountains of northwest Africa known as anonymi, or people without names. These small, isolated groups of people were described by Pliny, an ancient Roman historian.

- The Ojibway Indians of North America once considered it dangerous to speak the names of their own husbands and wives.

- Some Inuits take on a new name when they become old, hoping the name will give them renewed strength.

- The people of Indonesia may change their names after they have suffered some misfortune or have had a serious illness. They believe a new name will confuse the evil spirits that brought them grief.

IT'S A GIRL—NO, IT'S A BOY

The following names are given to both females and males. There might be slight differences in the spellings, but not in the pronunciation.

Ashley, Ashly	Jackie, Jacky	Lynne, Lynn
Berti, Berty	Jan	Marian, Marion
Billie, Billy	Jo, Joe	Martie, Marty
Bobbie, Bobby	Joyce	Merle, Myrle
Brooke, Brook	Karen, Karin	Nikki, Nicky
Carol, Carrol	Kelley, Kelly	Paige, Page
Carey, Cary	Kerrie, Kerry	Pat
Chris, Kris	Kim	Shelly, Shelley
Evelyn	Laverne, Lavern	Shirley
Frankie, Franky	Leigh, Lee	Stacy, Stacey
Gail, Gale	Leslie, Lesley	Teri, Terry
Gerry, Jerry	Lyle	Tracie, Tracy

NAMES FOR FEMALE ANIMALS

ANIMAL	FEMALE	ANIMAL	FEMALE
ANTELOPE	DOE	HORSE	MARE
BADGER	SOW	LEOPARD	LEOPARDESS
BEAR	SOW	LION	LIONESS
BUFFALO	COW	MOOSE	COW
CAMEL	COW	PIG	SOW
DOG	BITCH	POLECAT	JILL
ELEPHANT	COW	RABBIT	DOE
FOX	VIXEN	SHEEP	EWE
GOAT	NANNY	TIGER	TIGRESS

WORD WOMEN—EPONYMS

An eponym is a word or phrase derived from the name of a person. For example, ADA is the computer programming language named after Augusta Ada Lovelace of England who was the world's first computer programmer. Here are some other eponyms:

- An Annie Oakley is a free ticket to a show or a game. Annie Oakley was a sharpshooter who could shoot holes through a playing card when it was tossed into the air, making it look much like a punched ticket.

- Aphrodisiac comes from the name of the Greek goddess of love, Aphrodite.

- A Cassandra is someone who predicts disaster. Cassandra predicted the downfall of Troy in the story *The Illiad*.

- Fittonia is a flower named after the botanists Elizabeth and Sarah Fitton.

- Montessori is a method of education which stresses the development of a child's natural abilities and initiative. Maria Montessori developed this method and started the schools that teach it.

- A Pollyanna is a person who is blindly optimistic. Pollyanna was such a character in the novel *Pollyanna* by Eleanor Hodgman Porter.

- A Lucy Stoner is a woman who keeps her name after marrying. Lucy Stone was a nineteenth-century feminist who kept her name after marrying.

- Tawdry means showy or gaudy. The word comes

from St. Audrey, a seventeenth-century queen who wore lots of jewelry.

- A Victoria is a four-wheeled horse-drawn carriage for two. It was named after Queen Victoria of England.
- Xanthippe (pronounced zan-thip-ee) means an ill-tempered person. It comes from Xanthippe, who was married to Socrates.

NAME-O-RAMA

The royal record for the queen with the most middle names goes to Mary, wife of George V. Her middle names were Victoria, Augusta, Louisa, Olga, Pauline, Claudia, and Agnes.

Scarlett O'Hara was not the original name for the character in the novel *Gone with the Wind*. The author, Margaret Mitchell, had originally called her Pansy. Her editor suggested she come up with a different name, and Scarlett O'Hara was born.

Wendy is a name that was made up by J. M. Barrie for the older sister of the Darling family in the story of Peter Pan. It is said that Barrie devised the name because a friend's child had nicknamed him "Fwendie."

There are two U.S. states named after women: Maryland, named for Henrietta Maria, queen of Charles I of England; and Virginia, named for Elizabeth I of England, known as the Virgin Queen.

The most common last name in the world is Chang (Zhang), which is the name of more than 104 million people.

SLANGSTERS

These are expressions that use female names to describe either objects or human characteristics.

BARBIE DOLL	a mindless man or woman
BASEBALL ANNIE	a young female baseball fan
BIG BERTHA	a large woman
BLACK MARIA	a hearse
DUMB DORA	a stupid woman
NERVOUS NELLIE	a worrier
ETHEL	a coward, especially a cautious boxer
JANE DOE	the average woman
KATIE BAR THE DOOR	means trouble is at hand
LIZZIE	a beat-up car
SALLY ANN	a place that gives food and shelter
ZELDA	an uninteresting female

Jane Crow means discrimination against females. Most of these slang words are examples of Jane Crows.

PICK A NAME—ANY NAME

Your given name might be that of a flower, like Daisy, or a jewel, like Ruby, or a month, like April, or even a place, like Chelsea. If the meaning of your name is not so obvious, you might find its meaning here.

Alice (Alicia, Alisa, Allison)	*"noble princess"*
Alma	*"supportive, helpful"*
Amanda (Aimee, Amy)	*"loving, lovable"*
Amelia	*"hard working"*
Ann (Anita, Hannah, Nancy)	*"graceful"*
Barbara	*"strange, foreign"*
Brenda	*"fiery flaming sword"*
Caroline (Carla, Carrie)	*"noble spirited, strong"*
Catherine (Katy, Trina)	*"pure"*
Christine (Crystal, Tina)	*"fair Christian"*
Colleen	*"a girl"*
Cynthia	*"moon goddess"*
Darlene (Daryl)	*"dearly beloved"*
Deborah	*"the bee, industrious"*
Diana (Dinah)	*"goddess of the moon"*
Donna	*"lady"*
Elizabeth (Bess, Elisa, Liza)	*"consecrated to God"*
Emma	*"the healer"*
Eva (Eve, Evelyn)	*"life"*
Faye (Faith)	*"faithful"*
Frances (Chica, Francesca)	*"free"*
Genevieve	*"white wave"*
Gina	*"silvery"*
Gwendolyn	*"lady of the new moon"*
Helen (Eileen, Elaine, Eleanor)	*"light"*
Hilary	*"cheerful"*

Irene (Renata, Renee)	*"peace"*
Jane (Jeanne, Joan)	*"God's precious gift"*
Jessica	*"God's grace"*
Judith	*"admired, praiseworthy"*
Julia (Jill, Juliet)	*"youthful, soft-haired"*
Kathleen	*"beautiful eyes"*
Laura	*"laurel"*
Linda	*"beautiful"*
Louise (Eloise, Lois)	*"war hero"*
Lucille (Lucia, Lucy)	*"light, dawn"*
Margaret (Gretchen, Marjorie)	*"pearl"*
Mary (Marilynn, Molly)	*"bitter tears"*
Meghan	*"strong"*
Michelle	*"godly"*
Naomi	*"pleasant, sweet"*
Paula (Pauline)	*"little"*
Phoebe	*"brilliant"*
Rachel (Raquel)	*"innocent"*
Ramona (Mona)	*"protector"*
Roberta (Bobbie, Robin)	*"bright, famous"*
Ruth	*"beautiful friend"*
Sara (Sadie, Sally)	*"princess"*
Sophia (Fifi, Sonya)	*"wise"*
Stephanie	*"wearing a garland or crown"*
Susan	*"a lily"*
Teresa (Tracey, Tess)	*"harvester"*
Valerie	*"valiant, strong"*
Vivian	*"lively"*
Yolanda	*"modest, shy"*
Yvette (Yvonne)	*"archer"*
Zelda	*"unconquerable hero"*
Zora	*"dawn"*

SONG OF SONGS

Lots of songs have been written about women or include women's names in their titles. See if your name has been in a song...

NAME	SONG TITLE
ADELAIDE	"Adelaide's Lament"
ALICE	"Alice's Restaurant" "(In My Sweet Little) Alice Blue Gown"
ALLISON	"Allison"
AMY	"Once In Love with Amy"
ANNABEL	"Annabel Lee"
ANNABELLE	"Annabelle"
ANGELINA	"Angelina"
ANGIE	"Angie Baby" "Angie"
ANNIE	"Annie Get Your Gun" "Annie Laurie" "Annie's Song"
APRIL	"April Played the Fiddle"
BARBARA ANN	"Barbara Ann"
BEATRICE	"Beatrice Fairfax, Tell Me What to Do"
BERTHA	"Bertha"
BETTE	"Bette Davis Eyes"
BETTY LOU	"Betty Lou's Got a New Pair of Shoes" "Betty Lou is Coming Out"
BILLIE	"Billie Jean"
BONNIE	"My Bonnie Lies over the Ocean"
BRANDY	"Brandy"
BRIANNA	"Brianna"
CANDY	"Candy"
CAROLINE	"Sweet Caroline"
CATHY	"Cathy's Clown"

NAME	SONG TITLE
CECILIA	"Cecilia"
CINDY	"Cindy"
CLAIRE	"Planet Claire"
CLEMENTINE	"Clementine"
CORRINE	"Corrine, Corrine"
DAISY	"Daisy Bell"
DELILAH	"Delilah"
DINA	"Dina"
DINAH	"Dinah"
DOLORES	"Dolores"
DOMINIQUE	"Dominique, Dominique"
EILEEN	"Eileen"
ELEANOR	"Eleanor Rigby"
ELVIRA	"Elvira"
FRANKIE	"Frankie and Johnny"
GERTIE	"Gertie from Bizerte"
GIGI	"Gigi"
GLORIA	"Gloria"
HANNAH	"Miss Hannah"
HARRIET	"Harriet"
IDA	"Ida, Sweet as Apple Cider"
INEZ	"Mama Inez"
IRENE	"Goodnight Irene"
IRMA	"Irma La Douce"
IVY	"Ivy"
JACKIE	"(I Want to Be) Jackie Onassis"
JEANIE	"Jeanie with Light Brown Hair"
JESSIE	"Jessie's Girl"

NAME	SONG TITLE
JOANNA	"Joanna"
JUANITA	"Juanita"
JUDY	"Judy in Disguise"
KATE	"I Wish I Could Shimmy Like My Sister Kate"
KATHLEEN	"I'll Take You Home Again, Kathleen"
KATY	"K-K-K-Katy"
LAURA	"Laura"
LISA	"Mona Lisa"
LILY	"Hi Lili, Hi Lo"
LIZA	"Li'l Liza Jane"
LOUISE	"Louise"
LUCILLE	"Lucille"
LUCY	"Lucy in the Sky with Diamonds"
LULU	"Don't Bring Lulu"
MAGGIE	"Maggie May"
MANDY	"Mandy"
MARGIE	"Margie"
MARIA	"Maria"
MARY	"Mary's a Grand Old Name"
MARRIANE	"Marianne"
MARY LOU	"Mary Lou"
MATILDA	"Matilda" "Waltzing Matilda"
MAYBELLENE	"Maybellene"
MELISSA	"Melissa"
MELODY	"Melody"
MICHELLE	"Michelle"
MIMI	"Mimi"

NAME	SONG TITLE
NANCY	"Nancy (with the Laughing Face)"
NELLIE	"Wait till the Sun Shines, Nellie"
NOLA	"Nola"
NORMA	"Norma Jean"
PAULA	"Hey, Paula"
PATRICIA	"Patricia"
PEG	"Peg O' My Heart"
PEGGY SUE	"Peggy Sue"
RHONDA	"Help Me, Rhonda"
ROSALIE	"Rosalie"
ROSANNA	"Rosanna"
ROSE	"Ramblin' Rose" "Rose of Washington Square" "Second Hand Rose"
ROSIE	"Sweet Rosie O'Grady"
ROXANNE	"Roxanne"
RUBY	"Ruby Tuesday"
SALLY	"Long Tall Sally"
SHARONA	"My Sharona"
SHIRALEE	"Shiralee"
STEPHANIE	"Stephanie"
SUE	"Runaround Sue"
SUSANNA	"Oh Susanna"
SUSIE	"Wake Up, Little Susie" "If You Knew Susie Like I Know Susie"
SYLVIA	"Sylvia Speaks"
TESSIE	"Tessie, You Are the Only, Only, Only"
VALLERI	"Valleri"
VANESSA	"Vanessa"
YVETTE	"Dear Yvette"

TELL ME YOUR REAL NAME

Here are the real names of some famous women.

JULIE ANDREWS	Julia Wells
LAUREN BACALL	Betty Perske
ANNE BANCROFT	Annemarie Italiano
CHER	Cherilyn La Piere
JOAN CRAWFORD	Lucille Le Sueur
ANGIE DICKINSON	Angeline Brown
CRYSTAL GAYLE	Brenda Gayle Webb
RUTH GORDON	Ruth Jones
JEAN HARLOW	Harlean Carpenter
SUSAN HAYWARD	Edythe Marriner
JUDY HOLLIDAY	Judith Tuvim
JENNIFER JONES	Phyllis Isley
SOPHIA LOREN	Sofia Scicoloni
MADONNA	Madonna Louise Ciccone
JONI MITCHELL	Roberta Joan Mitchell
MARILYN MONROE	Norma Jean Baker
NINA SIMONE	Eunice Kathleen Waymon
MERYL STREEP	Mary Louise Streep
TINA TURNER	Annie May Bullock
TWIGGY	Lesley Hornby
TAMMY WYNETTE	Wynette Pugh

The following women took pseudonyms or pen names to conceal their gender. They believed that they couldn't get their work published because they were women. Maybe you know their assumed names:

- George Eliot was really Mary Ann Evans
- Currer Bell was really Charlotte Brontë
- Acton Bell was really Anne Brontë

- Ellis Bell was really Emily Brontë
- George Sand was really Amandine Dupin
- Michael Joseph was really Doris Lessing

WHAT'S THAT CELEBRITY KID'S NAME?

Here are the names of some daughters of well-known actors and singers.

Bill Cosby	*Evin*	Joan Lunden	*Jamie*
Cher	*Chastity*	Mick Jagger	*Jade*
Paul McCartney	*Mary, Stella*	Jack Nicholson	*Lorraine*
Mel Gibson	*Hannah*	Mia Farrow	*Daisy, Eliza, Gigi, Soon Yi*
Ted Danson	*Alexis*		

DAUGHTERS OF TIME

If your name is Tuesday it may be that you were born on that day. Let's look at some names that tell about the time of birth that are given to girls in Africa, Japan, and other places in the world.

Astrological names

Estrella is a name that means "child of the stars," referring to the stars of the zodiac. Many cultures have names for girls that refer to the astrological signs they were born under. Here are some astrological names from different cultures.

Aries	*Alala, Mesha*	Libra	*Asvina*
Taurus	*Taura*	Scorpio	*Belloma, Alima*
Gemini	*Dua*	Sagittarius	*Arcite*
Cancer	*Amaris, Candra*	Capricorn	*Capri*
Leo	*Ahira, Alzubra, Surya*	Aquarius	*Aria, Yolanda, Urania*
Virgo	*Aludra, Spica*	Pisces	*Mina*

Japanese names for girls:

Aki	born in Autumn	Asa	born in the morning
Haru	born in Spring	Cho	born at dawn
Watsu	born in summer	Sayo	born at night
Fuyu	born in winter		

Native American names for girls:

Muna	A Hopi name for girls born during the season when the streams rise.
Migina	An Omaha name that means "moon returning"
Mihuca	An Omaha name that means "loud voice moon"
Mitexi	An Omaha name that means "sacred moon"
Mitena	An Omaha name that means "new moon"

African names for girls:

Abimbola	born to be rich	Nombeko	respect
Aisha	life	Omorose	my beautiful child
Bahatti	luck	Talibah	seek after knowledge
Femi	love me	Tarana	Hausa name for a girl born during the day
Hasina	good		
Muteteli	dainty	Tisa	Swahili for "ninth born"
Ngozi	blessing		

There are eight days in the African Kalabari-Ijaw market week. Girls' names for these market days are:

Bene	born on Fenibene
Kaladoku	born on Ejibradokuene
Kalaobuta	born on Ejibrafeniobu
Doku	born on Opufedokuene
Obuta	born on Feniobu

Sports Special

WHEN THE FIRST OLYMPICS were held in ancient Greece, women were not even permitted to view the events. Today women are making and breaking Olympic records. When women were barred from competition, they climbed mountains or explored. It may have taken 4,000 years, but women have broken many barriers in sports.

Here are some of the many sports women have excelled in.

Adventure

- Gertrude Bell was born in England in 1868. She was the first European woman to travel in remote parts of the Middle East. She traveled, often alone, and wrote about her journeys and the excavations she saw. Because of her knowledge of the territory, the British government made her a diplomat in Baghdad in 1915.
- The first woman to cross Niagara Falls on a high wire was Maria Spelternia in 1876.
- The first European woman to travel to the forbidden city of Tibet was Alexandra David-Neel of England in 1924.
- Krystyna Choynowski-Liskiewicz of Poland was the first woman to sail around the world solo. She accomplished this feat on March 28, 1976.
- In 1979 Sylvia Earle became the first person in the world to dive to a depth of 1,250 feet. She led an all-woman team of scientists in an experiment in undersea living, staying for two weeks in a submerged capsule in the Caribbean Sea.
- In 1984 Soviet cosmonaut Svetlana Savitskaya became the first woman to walk in space.
- Tania Aebi was the first American woman and the youngest person ever to sail alone around the world. In 1985, at the age of 19, she undertook the 27,000-mile adventure on her twenty-six-foot sloop the *Varuna*. She returned to New York in 1987.
- Eileen Collins was the first woman to pilot a space shuttle mission, in February of 1995.

Angling (fishing)

- The first known essay on sports fishing was written by Dame Juliana Berners of Great Britain in 1406. She described how to make a rod and flies, when to fish, and the many kinds of fishing in her essay, "Treatise of Fishing with an Angle."
- B. Byer of Cape Moreton, Australia, caught a 1,052-pound white shark in 1954. It is the largest white shark ever caught by a woman to date.
- The International Women's Fishing Association of Palm Beach, Florida, was founded in 1955 to promote angling competitions for girls and women.

Archery

- The first international women's archery competition was held in 1931. Janina Spychajowa-Kurkowska of Poland won the women's singles title. She won six more world titles in archery, more than any other man or woman in history.
- Lida Howell of the U.S. won the most archery titles ever! Between 1883 and 1907 she won 17 National Women's Archery Championships.

Auto Racing

- The first all-women auto race took place in 1909. It was a roundtrip race from New York City to Philadelphia. There were twelve competitors. The Woman's Motoring Club cup went to Alice DiHeyes of New Jersey; she drove a Cadillac with four female passengers.
- The first girl to win the All-American Soap Box Derby was Karen Stead who won in 1975 at the age of eleven.
- Shirley "Cha-Cha" Muldowney was the first fe-

male licensed drag car racer in the United States in 1975. She was also the first woman to drive a quarter of a mile in under six seconds.

- The first woman to compete in the Indianapolis 500 auto race was Janet Guthrie in 1977.
- Maria-Teresa de Filippis of Italy was the first woman to compete in a European Grand Prix auto race, which she did in 1958.

Aviation

- In 1953 Jacqueline Cochran became the first woman to break the sound barrier. She was the founder of the WASPs (Women's Airforce Service Pilots), a female military organization established during World War II. She still holds more world aviation records than any other pilot, male or female.
- Bessie Coleman was the first African American aviator. She earned an international pilot's license in 1922. Nicknamed "Brave Bessie," she was dedicated to opening a flying school for young blacks when she died in a crash at age 33.
- Beryl Markham was born in England in 1902 and moved to Kenya in 1904. In 1936, after a career as a professional bush pilot in Africa, she realized her lifelong dream: She became the first person to fly solo west across the Atlantic Ocean. She flew from England to Nova Scotia in 21 hours and 25 minutes.
- Anne Morrow Lindbergh was the copilot and radio operator for her husband Charles Lindbergh when, in the 1930s, they flew their extraordinary and famous trip of 40,000 miles over

5 continents.

- Harriet Quimby (1884–1912) was the first licensed woman pilot in the U.S. and the first woman to fly across the English Channel. She was also a famous exhibition pilot and is responsible for coining the word "airline."
- In 1910 American Blanche Stuart Scott became the first woman to fly solo. She went on to be a stunt pilot and test flier until she was twenty-seven, when she retired and became a news commentator!
- Born in the U.S. in 1891, Katherine Stinson was a stunt flier and the first woman to "loop the loop." She was also the first woman to transport the U.S. mail by airplane.

Baseball

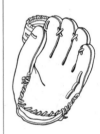

- Women have been playing baseball since 1866. Vassar College had the first women's baseball team.
- Lanny Moss was the first woman to manage a professional men's baseball team. In 1974 she was hired by the minor league Portland Mavericks.
- Girls were officially admitted to Little League on June 12, 1974.
- The first woman ever to sign a professional baseball contract was Jackie Mitchell when she signed with the Chattanooga Lookouts, a minor league team. She was a pitcher who is best remembered for striking out both Babe Ruth and Lou Gehrig in an exhibition game in 1931.
- Amanda Clement was the first official female umpire in men's baseball. She umpired from

1905–1911 for Midwestern semi-pro teams. She designed her own uniform, which was an ankle-length skirt, a white shirt with a black tie, and a baseball cap. She stored extra baseballs in her blouse. She later discarded the tie and had UMPS printed on the front of her uniform.

- The first woman owner of a major league team was Helene Britton, who owned the St. Louis Cardinals from 1911–1917.
- The first woman to pitch for a men's baseball team was Illa Borders. She began playing for Southern California College in Costa Mesa, California, in 1994.

Basketball

- The first women's intercollegiate basketball game took place between Stanford and the University of California on April 4, 1896. Stanford won.
- The Harlem Globetrotters are the only coed professional basketball team. In 1985 the team picked Olympian Lynette Woodward as its first female member.
- The U.S. Basketball Hall of Fame in Springfield, Massachusetts, began inducting members in 1959. It was not until 1992 that the first women were inducted. They are Nera White, a ten-time Most Valuable Player in Amateur Athletic Union tournaments in the 1950s and 1960s, and Lusia Harris-Stewart, a member of the first U.S. Olympic women's basketball team in 1976.
- The Women's Basketball Association, a professional basketball league, was founded in 1977. The WBA started with eight teams—Dayton,

New Jersey, New York, Houston, Milwaukee, Chicago, Iowa, and Minnesota—and lasted three seasons.

- Nancy Lieberman, the outstanding basketball player from Old Dominion College in Virginia, was the first woman to autograph a basketball marketed by a major sporting goods company (Spaulding).

Billiards

- Jean Balukas of Brooklyn, New York, began playing billiards when she was four years old and won her first national women's championship at the age of fourteen in 1959.

Bowling

- Bowling is the most popular sport for women in the United States today. Women first bowled in the 1880s, despite social disapproval.
- The first women's bowling tournament took place in 1917 in St. Louis, Missouri. There were 100 participants.
- Jennie Kelleher of Wisconsin was the first woman to bowl a perfect 300 game in 1930.
- More bowlers competed in the Women's International Bowling Congress Championship tournament in Reno, Nevada, in 1988 than in any other bowling match in the world. There were 77,735 women competitors.

Boxing

- In 1876, Nell Saunders defeated Rose Harland in the first United States women's boxing match. Saunders received a silver butter dish as a prize.

- In 1940 Belle Martel of Van Nuys, California, became the first woman boxing referee when she officiated at eight bouts in San Bernardino, California.
- The first woman to take part in the Golden Gloves boxing tournament was Marion Bermudez who boxed in Mexico City in 1975.
- The first woman boxing judge in the United States was Carol Polis. She was licensed in 1974.

Bullfighting

- Conchita Cintron was born in Chile in 1922 and began fighting bulls in Mexico at the age of fifteen. During her thirteen-year career she slew 800 bulls. She retired to live in Portugal in 1951.
- The first female professional bullfighter from the United States was Patricia McCormick. She made her debut in the ring on January 20, 1952 in Juarez, Mexico.

Croquet

- Croquet is believed to be the first outdoor game played by women and the first game in which men and women played together on an equal basis. The game came to the United States from England during the Civil War, and seemingly overnight became a very popular sport.
- The first women's croquet championship was held in England in 1869 and was won by Ms. Joad.

Cycling

- Cycling was included in the first modern Olympic games but it wasn't until 1984 that women were allowed to participate in this event.

- In Los Angeles at the 1984 Olympics, Connie Carpenter Finney of Madison, Wisconsin, won a medal for the United States for cycling. It was the first women's cycling medal won by the United States since 1912.
- In 1976, after winning three medals in speed skating at the Winter Olympics, Sheila Young of Michigan won both the United States and world sprint cycling titles.

Dogsledding

- Libby Riddles was the first woman to win the 1,135-mile Alaskan dogsled race, the Iditarod, in 1985. She mushed her thirteen-dog team across Alaska's ice fields and snowcapped mountains. It took her three weeks to make this grueling trek though blinding blizzards.
- Susan Butcher, the most famous female dogsled musher in the world, was a four-time winner of the Iditarod. She won the race in 1986, 1987, 1988, and 1990. She was named outstanding woman athlete of the world in 1989.

Fencing

- The first women's national fencing championship in the United States was held in 1912. Adeline Baylis won the competition.
- From 1932 to 1956 Ellen Muller-Preiss of Austria competed in every Olympic fencing competition. She won the gold medal in 1932 and the bronze from 1936 to 1948.

Field Hockey

- Constance M.K. Applebee is credited with bringing field hockey to the United States in 1901. She

had come from England to the U.S. to take a physical education course at Harvard University. The first game she organized was played on concrete with ice hockey sticks in a courtyard at Harvard.

- In 1922 women formed the United States Field Hockey Association.
- Field hockey was added to the Olympics in 1980. The Zimbabwe women's field hockey team went undefeated in the tournament to win the Olympic gold medal.

Football

- Pat Palinkas was the first woman to play in a professional football game. In 1970 she held the ball for the place kickers on the Orlando Panthers team.
- On December 27, 1987, Gayle Sierens became the first woman to do a play-by-play for a National Football League game, Kansas City vs. Seattle.

Golf

- Mary Queen of Scots was the first woman to play golf. It was during her reign that the famous golf course at St. Andrews was built, in 1552. Mary coined the term "caddy" by calling her assistants cadets.
- Patti Berg won the first Women's Open in 1946.
- The Ladies Professional Golf Association's player of the year from 1966 to 1973 (with the exception of 1970) was Kathy Whitworth of Texas. During her career, which lasted from 1962 to 1985, she won 88 championships, the best record of any professional woman golfer. She was inducted into

MARY QUEEN OF SCOTS

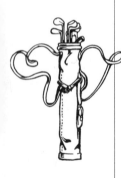

the LPGA Hall of Fame in 1975.

- Nancy Lopez was the first female golfer to win Rookie of the Year and Player of the Year in the same year. She won both these awards in 1978.
- In 1990 Juli Inkster of Los Altos, California, became the first woman to win the only professional golf tournament in the world in which women and men compete head-to-head. She won the Invitational Pro-Am at Pebble Beach in a one-stroke victory.

Gymnastics

- The first women's gymnastics instruction in the United States was given at Mount Holyoke College in 1862.
- Olympic gymnastics competition for women was introduced at the 1928 games.
- Larissa Latynina of Russia won 18 Olympic gymnastic medals, thus setting an Olympics record for women: nine gold medals, five silver, and four

bronze between 1956 and 1964.

- Marcia Frederick was the first American to win an Olympic gold medal and the gymnastics title. She won in 1973 on the uneven parallel bars.
- Olga Korbut of the Soviet Union inspired thousands of girls to take up gymnastics after she won two gold medals and one silver medal in the 1972 Olympics. She was later named Female Athlete of the Year.
- In the 1976 Olympics Nadia Comaneci of Romania became the first gymnast in Olympic history to score a perfect 10.0. She did this in the floor exercise.
- In 1984 16-year-old Mary Lou Retton of West Virginia became the youngest gymnast to win a gold medal. Her perfect performance on the vault earned her the Olympic gold medal in the Women's All-Around event.

Hockey

- On September 23, 1992, Manon Rheaume started as goalie for the Tampa Bay Lightning in a National Hockey League exhibition game. She was the first female goaltender to start a game in one of North America's four major professional sports leagues (baseball, football, basketball, and ice hockey).

Horse Racing

- The first woman jockey was Alicia Meynell of England. She first competed in a four-mile race in York, England, in 1804.
- In 1935 Mary Hirch became the first licensed female trainer of thoroughbred race horses.
- Julie Krone was the first female jockey to ride in

the Belmont Stakes, which is part of racing's Triple Crown. She rode in 1991. To date she is the winningest female jockey in history and one of the most successful jockeys of all time.

Horseshoe Pitching

- In 1920 Marjorie Voohies won the first national tournament for female horseshoe pitchers.

Mountain Climbing

- In 1906, at age forty-seven, Fanny Bullock Workman set a world climbing record for women of 22,815 feet when she reached the top of Pinnacle Peak in Nun Kun Massif in Kashmir.

- Annie Peck, an American schoolteacher, reached the 21,834-foot North Summit of Mt. Coropuna in Peru in 1911. The peak had never been scaled before. Peck was 58 years old at the time.

- Junko Tabei of Japan was the first woman in the world to reach the top of Mount Everest, the world's highest mountain. On May 16, 1975, leading an all-female Japanese expedition, she reached the summit. She has since climbed to the top of the highest mountains in 20 of the 167 countries of the United Nations. Her plan is to do the same in the remaining 147 United Nations countries.

- In 1989 Stacy Allison and Peggy Luce of Washington state became the first and second U.S. women to reach the top of Mt. Everest.

- Kitty Calhoun Grissom is the world's most famous living alpine climber. She specializes in ice and snow climbing. She was the first U.S. woman to scale Dhaulagiri, a 26,795-foot Himalayan peak.

Riding

- Women first competed with men in horseback riding in the Olympics in 1952. That year, Lis Hartel, who had retrained herself to ride after recovering from polio, won the silver medal at this event.

Running

Long-distance

- In 1967 Kathrine Switzer became the first woman ever to run in the famed Boston Marathon. Because it was a male-only event, she registered as K. Switzer and ran the entire route with officials attempting to tear her number from her back. Her run created such a stir that the AAU, the Amateur Athletic Union of the United States, rallied to get the rules changed. In 1972, after a long and hard five-year battle, Kathrine Switzer became the first woman to run officially and legally in the Boston Marathon.
- Grete Waitz of Norway has won the New York City Marathon nine times, more than any other competitor. She won in 1978, 1979, 1980, 1982, 1983, 1984, 1985, 1986, and 1988.

Short-distance

- Fanny Blankers-Koen of the Netherlands and Betty Cuthbert of Austria each have four Olympic gold medals, the most won by women runners. Fanny earned hers for the 100 meter, 200 meter, and 80 meter hurdles and the 4x100-meter relay in 1948. Betty earned golds in the 100 meter, 200 meter, and 4x100-meter relay in 1956 and the 400 meter in 1964.

- Chi Cheng of Taiwan was the first woman to run 100 yards in ten seconds flat. She accomplished this on June 13, 1970, in Portland, Oregon.
- Wilma Rudolph lost the use of her left leg when she was four. She wore a brace until she was eight years old and then a special shoe until she was eleven. Five years later she earned a place on the U.S. Olympic relay team that won her a bronze medal in 1956. She was the first woman ever to win 3 track and field gold medals at one Olympic Games. She earned the gold medals for the 100-, 200-, and 400-meter races in 1960.
- Florence Griffith Joyner, nicknamed "Flo-Jo," became the fastest woman in the world when at the 1988 Olympics she ran the 200 meter in 21:56.

Sailing

- Naomi James became the first woman to sail alone around the world; she made the trip in 1977 and 1978. She also set the record for the fastest round-the-world trip, making the journey in just under 272 days, breaking Sir Francis Chichester's record of 274 days.
- In 1994 twenty-three women were selected for the first all-female team to race for the America's Cup. They were: Stephanie Armitage-Johnson, Amy Baltzell, Shelley Beattie, Courtenay Becker, Sarah Bergeron, Merritt Carey, Sarah Cavanagh, Elizabeth Charles, Leslie Egnot, Christie Evans, Jennifer Isler, Diana Klybert, Linda Lindquist, Stephanie Maxwell-Pierson, Susanne Leech Nairn, Annie Nelson, Jane Oetking, Merritt Palm, Katherine Pettibone, Marci Porter,

Melissa Purdy, Hannah Swett, and Joan Lee Touchette.

Skating

Figure skating

- Theresa Weld Blanchard has achieved many figure skating firsts. She was the first U.S. national champion in 1914, won the first Olympic skating medal (bronze) for the U.S. in 1920, and won the U.S. pairs competition nine times with partner Nathaniel Niles.
- Tenley Albright was the first American woman figure skater to win both a skating world championship and an Olympic gold medal. She won the world championship in 1953 and the gold medal at the 1956 games.

- In 1964, at age 15, Peggy Fleming became the youngest person ever to win the U.S. women's figure skating championship. She won the only gold medal for the U.S. four years later at the 1968 Olympics at Grenoble, France.

Roller skating
- In 1976 Natalie Dunn became the first U.S. woman to win the world title in figure roller skating.

Speed skating
- Bonnie Blair became the all-time gold medal winner among U.S. female Olympic athletes after she won two gold medals at the 1994 Olympic Games in Lillehammer, Norway. She has won a total of five gold medals in her career.

Soccer
- In 1991 Jo Ann Fairbanks became the first American female referee to serve at an international soccer event when she was a lineswoman in the women's qualifying rounds for the North and Central American and Caribbean regional soccer tournament in Haiti.
- The first women's world soccer championship was won by the United States soccer team in December 1991.

Softball
- The first world softball championship was a women's tournament which was in held Melbourne, Australia, in 1965.
- Joan Joyce played basketball, volleyball, and softball as a teenager in Waterbury, Connecticut, but it was as a pitcher in softball that Joyce be-

came a legend. During twenty years of competition (1955–1975), she won 509 games and lost only 33.

- The first women's professional softball league, called the National Fastpitch Association, was recently formed and expects to play their first games in 1995.

Swimming

- Swimming became an Olympic event in 1908, but women weren't allowed to compete until 1912. Fanny Durack of Austria became the first female to win a gold medal for the 100-yard freestyle race that year.
- Gertrude Ederle was the first woman to swim the English Channel. In 1926 she swam from France to England in 14 hours and 39 minutes.
- Florence Chadwick was the first woman to swim both ways across the English Channel. In 1950 she swam from France to England in 13 hours, 20 minutes. In 1951 she swam from England to France.
- Donna de Varona of California is nicknamed the "Queen of Swimming." She won 37 championship titles and two Olympic gold medals in the 1960s. She excelled in freestyle, butterfly, breaststroke, and backstroke events.
- Tracy Caulkins, a swimmer from the University of Florida, won three gold medals in the 1984 Olympics. She won the 400-meter Individual Medley and the 200 Individual Medley, setting an Olympic record for time. She also won a medal for the 400-meter Team Medley. She retired from swimming at age twenty-one.

Table Tennis

- Ruth Hughes Aarons is the only American woman to win the world table tennis championship singles title. She won in 1936.

Tennis

- Mary Ewing Outerbride is credited with introducing lawn tennis to the United States in 1874.
- The first American woman to win the women's singles title at Wimbledon was May Sutton Bundy. She won in 1904 and in 1907. In 1930 she fractured her leg while playing at the U.S. Open at Forest Hills and finished her match using a crutch!
- Hazel Hotchkiss Wrightman is nicknamed the "Queen Mother of Tennis" because she dramati-

cally changed women's tennis. In 1903 in San Francisco, California, she introduced volley and net play. Prior to this the game was played from the baseline without much movement.

- Althea Gibson is credited with breaking the race barrier in tennis. In 1950 she became the first black woman to play at the prestigious USTA at Forest Hills.

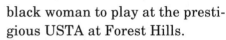

American athlete Babe Didrikson Zaharias earned more medals, broke more records, and swept more tournaments in more sports than any other athlete, male or female, in the twentieth century. She played forward with the Golden Cyclone Squad, one of the best girls' basketball teams in the country. At the 1932 Olympics she won gold medals in javelin throwing, 80-meter hurdles, and the high jump. From 1940 to 1950 she won every available golf title. In 1945 she was named Woman Athlete of the Year by a unanimous poll of Associated Press sportswriters. In 1956 she became the first winner of the American pro-golf title.

- Maureen "Little Mo" Connolly of the United States was the first woman to win the Grand Slam of tennis. In 1953 she won Wimbledon, the U.S. Open, the French Open, and the Australian Open. Only two other women have accomplished this feat: Margaret Court of Australia in 1970, and Steffi Graf of Germany in 1988.
- Tennis player Billie Jean King was one of the organizers of the 1970 Virginia Slims Tennis Tournament, the first tournament for women professional tennis players. The following year she became the first female athlete in any sport to earn more than $100,000 in a single season.
- Martina Navratilova is the winner of the most singles titles in a season. She won 16 in 1983. She retired from tennis in 1994.

Volleyball

- Inna Ryskal of the Soviet Union is the only woman to receive four Olympic medals for volleyball: a silver in 1964 and golds in 1968, 1972, and 1976.

Associated Press Female Athlete of the Year

YEAR	ATHLETE	SPORT
1931	Helene Madison	swimming
1932	Babe Didrikson	track
1933	Helen Jacobs	tennis
1934	Virginia Van Wie	golf
1935	Helen Wills Moody	tennis
1936	Helen Stephens	track
1937	Katherine Rawls	swimming
1938	Patty Berg	golf
1939	Alice Marble	tennis
1940	Alice Marble	tennis
1941	Betty Hicks Newell	golf
1942	Gloria Callen	swimming
1943	Patty Berg	golf
1944	Ann Curtis	swimming
1945	Babe Didrikson Zaharias	golf
1946	Babe Didrikson Zaharias	golf
1947	Babe Didrikson Zaharias	golf
1948	Fanny Blankers-Koen	track
1949	Marlene Bauer	golf
1950	Babe Didrikson Zaharias	golf
1951	Maureen Connolly	tennis
1952	Maureen Connolly	tennis
1953	Maureen Connolly	tennis
1954	Babe Didrikson Zaharias	golf
1955	Patty Berg	golf
1956	Patricia McCormick	diving
1957	Althea Gibson	tennis
1958	Althea Gibson	tennis
1959	Maria Bueno	tennis
1960	Wilma Rudolph	track
1961	Wilma Rudolph	track

YEAR	ATHLETE	SPORT
1962	Dawn Fraser	swimming
1963	Mickey Wright	golf
1964	Mickey Wright	golf
1965	Kathy Whitworth	golf
1966	Kathy Whitworth	golf
1967	Billie Jean King	tennis
1968	Peggy Fleming	skating
1969	Debbie Meyer	swimming
1970	Chi Cheng	track
1971	Evone Goolagong	tennis
1972	Olga Korbut	gymnastics
1973	Billie Jean King	tennis
1974	Chris Evert	tennis
1975	Chris Evert	tennis
1976	Nadia Comaneci	gymnastics
1977	Chris Evert	tennis
1978	Nancy Lopez	golf
1979	Tracy Austin	tennis
1980	Chris Evert Lloyd	tennis
1981	Tracy Austin	tennis
1982	Mary Decker Tabb	track
1983	Martina Navratilova	tennis
1984	Mary Lou Retton	gymnastics
1985	Nancy Lopez	golf
1986	Martina Navratilova	tennis
1987	Jackie Joyner-Kersee	track
1988	Florence Griffith Joyner	track
1989	Steffi Graf	tennis
1990	Beth Daniel	golf
1991	Monica Seles	tennis
1992	Monica Seles	tennis
1993	Sheryl Swoopes	basketball
1994	Bonnie Blair	speed skating

Women of Influence

POWER AND INFLUENCE ARE human domains. Both women and men have ruled countries, influenced religions, and fought wars. However, the roles women have played in history have often been minimalized or even forgotten. So let's turn the spotlight on influential and powerful women throughout history.

WOMEN WHO LEFT THEIR "STAMPS" ON HISTORY

Each of the following forty-seven women have made a significant contribution to society. As a result, they have been pictured on United States postage stamps.

The only woman to appear on U.S. currency is Susan B. Anthony. The U.S. mint first made the Susan B. Anthony one-dollar coin in 1979.

NAME	YEAR ISSUED	CONTRIBUTION
Queen Isabella of Spain	1893	Her patronage of Christopher Columbus made his trips to the New World possible.
Martha Washington	1902	First First Lady of the United States
Pocahontas	1907	The Powhatan princess who saved the life of Captain John Smith.
Molly Pitcher	1928	Mary Hayes McCauley earned the name Molly Pitcher by carrying water to the men in the battle of Monmouth in 1778.
Susan B. Anthony	1936, 1955	Feminist who spent more than fifty years fighting for women's rights.
Virginia Dare	1937	First child born on American soil, in 1587.
Louisa May Alcott	1940	American author famous for her books *Little Women* and *Little Men*.
Frances E. Willard	1940	Educator, reformer, lecturer, and women's suffrage supporter.
Jane Addams	1940	Founder of Hull House in Chicago, a social welfare center.
Clara Barton	1948	Founded the American Red Cross.
Juliette Gordon Low	1948	Founded the Girl Scouts of America.
Moina Michael	1948	Initiated the Veterans of Foreign Wars fundraising drive, selling red poppies in 1915.

NAME	YEAR ISSUED	CONTRIBUTION
Betsy Ross	1952	America's most famous flagmaker.
Sacajawea	1954	Shoshone guide who led the Lewis and Clark expedition of 1804.
Amelia Earhart	1963	First woman to fly solo, nonstop across the Atlantic Ocean.
Eleanor Roosevelt	1930, 1984	American diplomat, writer, social reformer and First Lady to Franklin D. Roosevelt.
Mary Cassatt	1966, 1988	American painter best known for her works of mothers and children.
Lucy Stone	1968	Nineteenth century abolitionist and women's rights leader.
Grandma Moses	1969	Anna Mary Robertson Moses took up painting at the age of 76. She continued to paint until her death at age 101.
Emily Dickinson	1971	American poet who wrote more than 1,700 poems.
Willa Cather	1973	Pulitzer Prize–winning novelist.
Dr. Elizabeth Blackwell	1973	First woman physician in the U.S.
Sybil Ludington	1975	Sixteen-year-old Revolutionary War hero.
Clara Maass	1976	Twenty-five-year-old U.S. Army nurse who advanced medical science when she volunteered to be bitten by a mosquito carrying yellow fever.
Harriet Tubman	1978	Leader of the Underground Railroad, which brought slaves to freedom.
Frances Perkins	1980	First woman member of the presidential Cabinet (Secretary of Labor) appointed by F.D. Roosevelt.

EMILY DICKINSON

NAME	YEAR ISSUED	CONTRIBUTION
Dolley Madison	1980	First Lady who saved White House treasures during the capture of the capital by the British in 1814.
Emily Bissell	1980	Leader in the fight against tuberculosis who introduced Christmas seals in the United States.
Helen Keller and Anne Sullivan	1980	Famous student who overcame tremendous handicaps, and her extraordinary teacher
Edith Wharton	1980	Pulitzer Prize–winning novelist known for her novels *Ethan Frome* and *The Age of Innocence.*
Dorothea Dix	1983	Nineteenth-century crusader for the poor and mentally handicapped.
Pearl S. Buck	1983	Author of more than 100 books, she was awarded the Pulitzer Prize for *The Good Earth.*
Rachel Carson	1981	The publication of her book *Silent Spring* in 1961 touched off a major controversy over the effects of pesticide.
Lillian M. Gilbreth	1984	Engineering pioneer who analyzed how tasks are done, hoping to increase the efficiency of workers.
Edna St. Vincent Millay	1981	American poet whose work was first published when she was just fourteen years old.
Mildred (Babe) Didrikson Zaharias	1981	One of the greatest athletes of the twentieth century. She excelled in track, golf, baseball, and basketball.
Dr. Mary Walker	1982	Devoted herself to the care and treatment of the sick and wounded during the Civil War.
Mary McLeod Bethune	1985	Educator and social activist who founded the Daytona Educational and Industrial Training School for Negro Girls, currently known as Bethune-Cookman College.

NAME	YEAR ISSUED	CONTRIBUTION
Abigail Adams	1985	First Lady to John Adams, she influenced American politics through her letters to her husband.
Sojourner Truth	1986	Born Isabella Baumfree, she was the first black woman to speak publicly against slavery.
Belva Ann Lockwood	1986	First woman candidate for president.
Margaret Mitchell	1986	Pulitzer Prize–winning author best known for *Gone with the Wind*.
Mary Lyon	1987	Education pioneer who founded Mount Holyoke College.
Julia Ward Howe	1987	Composer of "The Battle Hymn of the Republic."
Hazel Wightman	1990	Olympic gold medalist credited with doing more to build American and international women's tennis than any other player.
Helene Madison	1990	A gold medalist in the 1932 Olympic Games.
Ida Wells	1990	Civil rights activist who cofounded the National Association for the Advancement of Colored People.
Marianne Moore	1990	Poet who won the Pulitzer Prize in 1951 for her *Collected Poems*.
Blanche Stuart Scott	1980	First American woman to receive a pilot's license.
Harriet Quimby	1991	First American woman pilot to fly the English Channel.
Nellie Cushman	1994	The "Angel of Tombstone," an anti-violence advocate who raised orphans and campaigned against public hanging. She lived from 1849 to 1925.
Marilyn Monroe	1995	American film actor.

POWER POINTS

Did you know these facts about powerful women?

Queen Elizabeth II of Great Britain has had the longest reign of any queen ruling today. She became queen in 1952.

- In prehistoric times, women were worshiped as supernatural beings because they could create life. The supreme creator was female—the Great Goddess, who reigned from 7000 B.C. to the closing of the last Goddess temples in 500 A.D.

- In the tenth and eleventh centuries a succession of seventeen women known as the Habe Queens ruled Daura. Daura is in what is now northern Nigeria. Their names were:

Kurfuru	*Batatume*	*Zama*
Shata	*Yanbamu*	*Yakumo*
Gino	*Innagari*	*Yukuna*
Walzama	*Gamata*	*Gizirgizir*
Shawata	*Sandamata*	*Hamata*
Daura	*Jamata*	

- The Iroquois, Navajo, and Hopi women played a special role in their tribes. The older and wiser women chose the *sachem,* or chief, who ruled the tribe. Though they themselves did not govern, the women were in control even after a chief had been chosen because the women had the power to initiate proceedings to depose the chief if he failed to perform his duties. The women also ran the treasury, which consisted of resources such as corn, furs, fresh dried and smoked meats, and strings and belts of wampum.

There are six reigning queens in Europe today. They are the royalty in those countries, but the governments are separate.

- *Queen Elizabeth II— Great Britain*
- *Queen Sofia—Spain*
- *Queen Beatrix— The Netherlands*
- *Queen Margrethe II— Denmark*
- *Queen Silvia—Sweden*
- *Queen Fabiola— Belgium*

There have been many talented rulers:

- Queen Margrethe II of Denmark is a well-known illustrator. Her work appears in a recent edition of *The Lord of the Rings* by J.R.R. Tolkien.
- Queen Beatrix of the Netherlands is an accomplished sculptor.
- Queen Liliuokalani of Hawaii wrote the famous song "Aloha Oe."
- Burmese women have enjoyed equality with men throughout history. Inscriptions in pagan temples refer to female writers, scholars, musicians, and chiefs.

First Women Firsts

1960   Siramavo Bandaranaike of Sri Lanka became the first woman to head up a modern nation.

1974   Isabelita Perón was the first woman ruler in South America.

1980   Vigdis Finnbogadóttir was the first woman to be elected president in Iceland.

1987   Mary Eugenia Charles, a former slave, was the first female elected prime minister in Dominica.

1988   Lenora Fulani was the first woman and first black presidential candidate to get on the ballot in all fifty U.S. states.

1990   Violeta Barriosde Chamorro was the first woman to be elected president in Nicaragua.

1994   Sharon Sayles Belton became the first woman and the first African American to serve as mayor of Minneapolis, Minnesota.

WOMEN ON PEDESTALS

These are monumental women! Because of their achievements, their likenesses have been carved in stone for all to see and remember. Not all great women have been remembered this way, but those Americans who have can be found right here.

Who: Katharine Lee Bates, author of "America the Beautiful"
What: Six-foot-two-inch bronze statue showing her at the top of Pikes Peak, where she was inspired to write the song.
Where: Falmouth, Massachusetts, her birthplace.

Who: Mary McLeod Bethune, educator
What: Seventeen-foot bronze statue with arms outstretched to two young children and inscribed with the words, "I leave you love, I leave you hope...I leave you racial dignity."
Where: Washington, D.C.

Who: Mary Ann Bickerdyke, Civil War relief worker for the North
What: A stone statue of "Mother Bickerdyke" giving a drink to a wounded soldier with an inscription of the base of the statue which says: "'She outranks me'—General Sherman."
Where: Galesburg, Illinois.

Who: Alice Cogswell, first student at the first school for the deaf in the U.S.
What: Young Alice is shown signing the letter A with her teacher Thomas Hopkins Gallaudet.
Where: Gallaudet University, Washington, D.C.

Who: Jane Delano, founder of the Red Cross Nurs-

ing Service
What: A statue representing all nurses, named the Jane Delano Monument.
Where: Washington, D.C.

Who: Mary Dyer, martyr for religious freedom
What: A statue of Mary Dyer by Quaker artist Sylvia Shaw Judson.
Where: Boston, Massachusetts

Who: Amelia Earhart, pioneer aviator, called the "Golden Girl of Aviation"
What: A seven-foot-tall statue covered with gold leaf, with airplane propellers embedded in the base.
Where: North Hollywood, California

Who: Laura Haviland, Quaker abolitionist, founder of the Raisin Institute for fugitive slaves
What: A statue showing her seated with her book, *A Woman's Life Work.*
Where: Adrian, Michigan

Who: Mary Jemison was captured by Seneca Indians and then chose to stay with them. When she was 80 years old, she told of her adventures in the best-selling book *The Life of Mary Jemison.*
What: A life-size bronze statue.
Where: Castile, New York

Who: Mother Joseph, who established more than two dozen hospitals, schools, and orphanages in the Northwest.
What: A small bronze statue showing Mother Joseph kneeling in prayer.

Where: Vancouver, Washington

Who: Annie Louise Keller, who in 1927 risked her life to save a classroom full of children from a tornado.
What: A pink marble sculpture of her protecting a child.
Where: White Hall, Illinois

Who: Queen Liliuokalani, last queen of Hawaii

What: An eight-foot tall statue of her holding the constitution of Hawaii in one hand and a page of the traditional Hawaiian farewell song, "Aloha Oe," which she wrote, in the other.
Where: Honolulu, Hawaii

Who: Sybil Ludington, 16-year-old Revolutionary War hero
What: Bronze statue showing her on horseback to portray her nighttime ride to warn soldiers.
Where: Carmel, New York

Who: Edith Graham Mayo, wife of the cofounder of the Mayo Clinic and its first nurse.
What: Small bronze statue showing Edith in her nurse's uniform.
Where: Rochester, Minnesota

Who: Annie Moore, 15-year-old from Ireland who was the first immigrant to pass through the receiving room at Ellis Island when it opened in 1892.
What: Bronze statue showing Annie with a satchel in her hand and a hopeful expression on her face.

Where: Ellis Island, New York Harbor, New York

Who: Esther Morris, who helped make Wyoming the first state to grant women the right to vote.
What: A shiny brass statue showing her as a young woman carrying flowers and a portfolio.
Where: Entrance to the Capitol Building, Cheyenne, Wyoming

Who: Annie Oakley (Phoebe Anne Mozee), famous Wild West sharpshooter
What: A life-size bronze statue showing her standing, holding her rifle by her side.
Where: Greenville, Ohio

Who: Lottie Holman O'Neill, first woman elected to the Illinois legislature.
What: Statue installed in a niche in the Capitol Building rotunda.
Where: Springfield, Illinois

Who: Pocahontas, who at the age of 10 helped the Jamestown colonists and saved the life of their leader, Captain John Smith.
What: A life-size outdoor statue showing her with open, helping arms.
Where: Jamestown, Virginia

Who: Eleanor Roosevelt, First Lady, humanitarian
What: Eight-foot bronze statue of her as an older woman leaning against a rock.
Where: Riverside Park, New York City

Who: Florence Sabine, pioneering physician and advocate of public health laws

The nation's first public statue of a First Lady was of Eleanor Roosevelt.

There are a record-breaking five statues of the brave Shoshoni guide Sacajawea erected throughout the U.S.

What: Replica of the bronze statue in the national Statuary Building which depicts her sitting on a lab stool with a microscope close at hand.
Where: Denver, Colorado

Who: Sacajawea, guide and scout for the Lewis and Clark expedition.
What: Twelve-foot bronze statue showing Sacajawea with her baby strapped to her back.
Where: Bismarck, North Dakota

Who: Maria Sanford, pioneer, educator, and civic leader
What: Seven-foot bronze statue with an inscription on the base calling her "the best known and best loved woman in Minnesota."
Where: Statuary Hall, U.S. Capitol Building, Washington, D.C.

Who: Samantha Smith, ambassador for peace between the U.S. and the U.S.S.R. when she was 10 years old. She died at the age of 13 in a plane crash while returning to Maine from Europe.
What: Bronze statue showing her posed with a dove of peace and proclaiming her "Maine's young ambassador of goodwill."
Where: State Capitol, Augusta, Maine

Who: Statue of Liberty, the most famous symbolic statue of a woman, modeled after Marie Bartholdi, the sculptor's mother.
What: 151-foot copper figure of a woman draped in a loose robe, holding a torch in her uplifted right hand and a tablet with the date of the Declaration of Independence in Roman numerals in her left. Installed in 1886.

Where: Liberty Island, New York Harbor, New York

Who: Gertrude Stein, author
What: Bronze statue showing her seated in the way she once described herself as looking "like a great Jewish Buddha."
Where: Bryant Park, New York

Who: We-no-nah, Indian woman who, according to legend, drowned rather than marry a warrior of her father's choice.
What: Bronze likeness showing her in a long dress with buckskin fringe and a traditional sun ornament on her left shoulder.
Where: Winona, Minnesota, the city named after her.

Who: Phillis Wheatley, famous slave poet
What: Bronze statue by Elizabeth Catlett, dedicated by black female poets.
Where: Jackson, Mississippi

Who: Emma Willard, women's educator.
What: Statue depicting her seated in her favorite chair with a book in her right hand.
Where: Outside the Emma Willard School, Troy, New York

Who: Women's Rights Leaders
What: A grouping of nineteen life-size bronze statues of women and men who attended the world's first women's rights convention. Among them are Lucretia Mott, Elizabeth Cady Stanton, and Jane Hunt.
Where: National Historical Park, Seneca Falls, New York

GUIDE TO WORLDWIDE GODDESSES

"Mothers of the Earth," "Queens of the Universe," "Queens of the Heavens," all are goddesses believed to be creators, lawmakers, prophets, healers, hunters, battle leaders, and truth-givers. Let's go back in time around the world and identify some important goddesses.

North America

Most Indian tribes believe that life originated from females. They also believe that all spirits that are life-giving forces, such as rain and corn, are brought forth from female deities.

- Sedna. She ruled over the sea animals. The Inuits (Eskimos) believed that she used ugliness as protection. Anyone who dared to look at her would be struck dead.
- Selu. The Corn Mother of the Cherokee who cut open her breast so that corn could spring forth and give life to the people.
- Blue Corn Woman and White Corn Maiden. For the Tewa Pueblo people these were the first mothers. Blue was the summer mother; White was the winter mother.
- Three Sisters. In the Iroquois tradition, the life-giving forces of corn, beans, and squash were given by the Three Sisters, who were thanked daily.
- White-painted Mother. White-painted Mother is the mother of Child of the Water, from whom all Apaches are descended. She keeps her child safe in her womb, slays all evil monsters, and keeps the world safe for Apaches.
- White Buffalo Calf Woman. For the Lakota,

White Buffalo Calf Woman is the giver of the Pipe. The Pipe represents truth.

China
- The Chinese goddess Ma-Ku personifies the goodness in all people. She took land from the sea and planted it with mulberry trees. She freed the slaves from her cruel father.
- Kuan Yin represents wisdom and purity for the Chinese. She had a thousand arms, symbolizing her infinite compassion.

Egypt
- Nut represents the heavens. Her body was covered with speckles which were the stars. She existed before all else had been created.
- Isis invented agriculture. She was the god of law, healing, and fertility.
- Hathor protected all things feminine.
- Tefnut was the god of the dew.

Ancient Greece and Rome
- Aphrodite was the Greek god who brought and maintained love in the world. Her Roman name was Venus.
- Artemis was the Greek god who ruled over the hunt and over women in childbirth. Her Roman name was Diana.
- Athena was the Greek god of crafts, war, and wisdom. Her Roman name was Minerva.
- Demeter was the Greek god who made all things grow. Her Roman name was Ceres.
- Gaea was the Greek god of the earth. Her Roman name was Terra.
- Hera was the Greek protector of marriage and

women. Her Roman name was Juno.

- Hestia was the Greek god of the hearth and home. Her Roman name was Vesta.
- Eos was the Greek god of the dawn. It was thought that she emerged every day from the ocean and rose into the sky on a chariot drawn by horses. The morning dew represented her tears of grief for her slain son.

Hawaii

- Pele is the powerful Hawaiian god of fire. She lived in the Kilauea Volcano and ruled over the family of fire gods. When she was angry she would erupt and pour fiery rock over the land.
- Hiiaka is the youngest sister of Pele. She is a fierce warrior and yet a kind and calm friend of humanity. She gave people the healing arts, creative arts, and the gift of storytelling.

Ireland

- Danu was the mother of the Tuatha De Danann, the most important race of people in Celtic mythology.
- Brigit gave the Irish their language.
- The Irish god Cerrid gave intelligence and knowledge to humans.
- Caillech was the wisest woman. She could move mountains and was thought to be the daughter of the moon.

Scandinavia

- Freyja was the god of love and beauty.
- Hel ruled the underworld.
- Norns were three sisters who lived around the tree of life. They controlled the past, present, and future.

WOMEN RULERS OF THE WORLD

Throughout history and around the world, many women have ruled their countries. There are also many women leaders today. In many cases, the queens alive and in power today do not actually rule their countries; they are symbolic rulers only and are not listed here. Instead, here is a list of actual female rulers, the countries in which they rule or ruled, and the dates they reigned.

When a ruler abdicates her position, it means she gives it up peacefully. When a ruler is deposed, it means she is forcibly removed from power.

COUNTRY	NAME	REIGN
Argentina	President Isabelita Perón	1974–1976
Lesser Armenia	Queen Zabel	1219–1226
Bolivia	Prime Minister Lidia Gueiler	1979–1980
Burundi	Prime Minister Sylvie Kinigi	1993–present
Byzantium (Roman Empire)	Empress Theodora	1055–1056
Cambodia	Queen Kossamak (joint ruler)	1955–1960
Canada	Prime Minister Kim Campbell	1993 (4 months)
Central African Republic	Prime Minister Elizabeth Domitien	1974–1976
China	Empress Wu Chao Empress Tsu-Hsi	655–705 1875–1879, 1898–1908
Dominica	Prime Minister Mary Eugenia Charles	1980–present
Denmark	Queen Margaret Queen Margrethe II	1387–1412 1972–present
Egypt	Queen Hatshepsut Queen Eje Queen Arsinoe II (joint ruler) Queen Berenice Queen Cleopatra VII	1501–1498 B.C. 1351–1350 B.C. 279–270 B.C. 81–80 B.C. 51–50 B.C.
Ethiopia	Empress Waizero	1916–1930
France	Prime Minister Edith Cresson	1991–1992

COUNTRY	NAME	REIGN
Great Britain	Queen Jane (Lady Jane Grey)	1553 (9 days)
	Queen Mary I	1553–1558
	Queen Elizabeth I	1558–1603
	Queen Mary II (joint ruler)	1689–1702
	Queen Anne	1702–1714
	Queen Victoria	1837–1901
	Queen Elizabeth II	1952–present
	Prime Minister Margaret Thatcher	1979–1990
Haiti	Provisional President Erita Pascal-Trouillot	1990
Hungary	Queen Mary	1382–1387
	Queen Elizabeth	1439–1440
	Queen Maria Theresa	1740–1780
Iceland	President Vigdis Finnbogadóttir	1980–present
India	Prime Minister Indira Gandhi	1966–1977 1980–1984
Ireland	President Mary Robinson	1990–present
Israel and Judah	Queen Athaliah	842–837 B.C.
	Prime Minister Golda Meir	1969–1974
Italy	Queen Theodelinda	590
	Queen Joanna I of Naples	1343–1381
	Queen Maria of Sicily	1377–1402
	Queen Joanna II of Naples	1414–1435
Japan	Empress Suiko Tenno	593–628
	Empress Kogyoku	642–645
	Empress Jito	686–697
	Empress Gemmyo	703–724
	Empress Koken (abdicated)	749–758
	Empress Shotuku-Koken	764–770
Lithuania	Prime Minister Kazimicra Prunskiene	1990–1992
Madagascar	Queen Ranavalona I	1828–1861
	Queen Rasoaherina	1863–1868
	Queen Ranavalona II	1868–1883
	Queen Ranavalona III (deposed)	1883–1896
Netherlands	Queen Wilhelmina (abdicated)	1890–1948
	Queen Juliana	1948–1980
Nicaragua	President Maria Liberia Peres	1984–1985
	President Violeta Barriosde Chamorro	1990–present

**QUEEN
ELIZABETH I**

QUEEN VICTORIA

COUNTRY	NAME	REIGN
Norway	Queen Margaret	1387–1412
	Prime Minister Groharlem Brundtlandt	1981 and 1986
Pakistan	Prime Minister Benazir Bhutto	1988–1990
Philippines	Maria Corazon Aquino	1986–1992
Poland	Queen Hedwige	1384–1399
	Prime Minister Hanna Suchocka	1992–1993
Portugal	Queen Maria I	1777–1816
	Queen Maria II	1826–1828
	Queen Maria III	1834–1853
	Prime Minister Maria de Lourdes Pintasilgo	1979 (149 days)
Roman Empire	Empress Irene	797–802
Russia	Queen Tamara	1184–1212
	Empress Catherine I	1725–1727
	Empress Anna Ivanovna	1730–1740
	Empress Elizabeth Petrovna	1741–1762
	Empress Catherine II (The Great)	1762–1796
Scotland	Queen Mary Stuart (executed)	1542–1567
Seminole Nation	Betty Mae Jumper	1960–1969
Spain	Queen Dona Urraca	1109–1126
	Queen Juana I	1274–1307
	Queen Juana II	1328–1349
	Queen Dona Blanca	1425–1441
	Queen Isabel I (joint ruler)	1474–1504
	Queen Catalina de Albret	1481–1512
	Queen Isabel II	1833–1868
Sri Lanka	Queen Anula	47–42 B.C.
	Queen Sivali	35 B.C.
	Queen Lalavati	1197–1200
	Queen Kalyanavati	1202–1208
	Queen Lilavati (restored)	1209–1212
	Prime Minister Sirimavo Bandaranaike	1960–1965, 1970–1977
Sweden	Queen Christina (abdicated)	1632–1654
	Queen Ulrica Eleonora (abdicated)	1718–1720
Tonga	Queen Salote Tubou III	1918–1965
Turkey	Prime Minister Tansu	1993–present

EMPRESS CATHERINE I

QUEEN ISABEL II

WOMEN IN THE HOUSE

Here are some facts about women who have served or are currently serving in the U.S. Congress.

- There have been 163 women elected or appointed to the U.S. Congress. Jeannette Rankin, Republican from Montana, was the first woman elected to serve in Congress. On November 9, 1916, she was elected to the House of Representatives as Montana's Representative-at-Large to the 65th Congress; she served from 1917 to 1919. Since that time 162 other women have served in Congress.

- There were a record number of women serving in the 103rd Congress: 48 in the House and 7 in the Senate. Carol Moseley-Braun, a Democrat from Illinois and one of the newest Senators, was the first black woman and the first black Democrat to serve.

- There have been 144 women elected to the House of Representatives. Of these, 32 were elected to fill vacancies caused by their husbands' deaths. Fifteen were then elected to additional terms.

- Edith Nourse Rogers, Republican from Massachusetts, holds the record for the longest service by a woman in the House of Representatives. Originally elected to fill the vacancy caused by her husband's death, she served from June 25, 1925, until her death on September 10, 1960.

- Representative Ileana Ros-Lehtineor, a Republican from Florida, was first elected in 1989. She is the first Hispanic woman and first Cuban American to serve in Congress. Representative Nydia Velazquez, a Democrat from New York, was elected in 1992 and became the first Puerto Rican woman to serve in Congress.

EMILY's list (Early Money Is Like Yeast) is a political network to help women democrats get elected to political office in the U.S.

WISH List (Women In the Senate and House) is an organization that supports pro-choice Republican female candidates for Congress and governorships by contributing time or money to their campaigns.